PRISON | RIOTS | PARAMILITARIES | MURDER | PEACE

A Child of The TROUBLES

Alex (Oso) Calderwood

"Staying down was not an option."
Oso

A Child of the Troubles

Copyright © 2022 by Alex Calderwood

ISBN: 978-1-915223-14-2

All rights reserved.
No part of this publication may be reproduced, stored in a retrieval system, or transmitted in any form or by any means, electronic, mechanical, photocopying or otherwise, without prior written consent of the publisher except as provided by under United Kingdom copyright law. Short extracts may be used for review purposes with credits given.

Scripture taken from the New King James Version®. Copyright © 1982 by Thomas Nelson. Used by permission. All rights reserved.
Scripture quotations marked (NIV) are taken from the Holy Bible, New International Version®, NIV®. Copyright © 1973, 1978, 1984, 2011 by Biblica, Inc.™ Used by permission of Zondervan. All rights reserved worldwide. www.zondervan.com The "NIV" and "New International Version" are trademarks registered in the United States Patent and Trademark Office by Biblica, Inc.™

Published by

Maurice Wylie Media
Your Inspirational & Christian Publisher

For more information visit
www.MauriceWylieMedia.com

Contents

	Page
Today I met a man	9
Introduction	11
Chapter 1 – 'Have You Got a Gun?'	13
Chapter 2 – Troubled Times & the Three Scottish Soldiers	25
Chapter 3 – Sleeping with Your Enemy	34
Chapter 4 – Paramilitaries Became My Family	42
Chapter 5 – Hydebank Youth Prison	53
Chapter 6 – Time on Your Hands	60
Chapter 7 – The Road to The Maze (H-Block)	70
Chapter 8 – The Maze, a Training Camp	77
Chapter 9 – No More Orders	88
Chapter 10 – A New Lease of Life	97
Chapter 11 – A Downward Spiral	106
Chapter 12 – Seeds of Hope	116
Chapter 13 – The Prodigal Returns	123
Contact	133

Today I met a man

Today I met a man, who spoke the truth
Who spoke with the fragmentation of his youth
Of a land of conflict and judgement misplaced
Preconceived ideas destroying a race
But he held high his head and he talked of the day
That through the confusion, he took life away
It wasn't a sentimental tale and pity had no place
It was a humbling story of a God full of grace
A simple reminder that sin has no size
of the quality we share if we look through God's eyes
We are each of us guilty, but blameless through grace
Each of us saved through shame and disgrace
Today I met a man who spoke the truth, but spoke it out just as it is
In the knowledge that God's forgiveness is his

(Dedicated to Alex (Oso) Calderwood)[1]

---

1 Story told within the book.

Introduction

Today, when I walk down the Shankill Road in Belfast, I see happy faces going about their everyday lives. But I still see pain as well — hidden hurt buried within; trauma of the past. The rioting might have stopped and a kind of law and order may have resumed, but many have lost loved ones. Every face that walks the streets of the Protestant Shankill and the Catholic Falls has a story to tell.

How do they continue to live with the trauma of their loss? What stories will they tell their children?

My name is Alex Calderwood, or Oso to my friends. I am one who has not only lived through the Troubles of Northern Ireland, but I became caught up in the conflict. The story of my upbringing is not the one that a mother wishes upon her child; neither is it one that I would wish upon any generation.

I invite you to step into my shoes for a wee while. Experience the story of my childhood. Journey with me through my life. But remember just one thing — I am human, I make choices, not always the right ones as you'll read. But, I'm just like you. I want to be loved; to have a family around me who care. Most importantly, I want to make a difference. I want to share with you, my reader, that regardless of what life throws at you, you can be an overcomer. You can bring change to every situation. You can bring life and hope to others. Even when you have done wrong, there is still hope. You can get up off your feet, brush the dust off and say, *Today is a new day.*

I have discovered that there is a God who forgives, cleanses, heals and restores. And if God can forgive me, he can forgive you. If I can be given a fresh page on which to start again, and then yes, again if I need to, then you can too.

I recognise that I am still a work in progress. I take each day as it comes and treat it as a gift and a blessing. My desire is to reach out and help others and for those searching for answers, I want to show where there is life — there is hope. I pray you will not make the same mistakes I did.

Chapter 1

"Have You Got a Gun?"

My street had become a war zone. People were fighting against each other. People were killing each other. Fear became a dominant factor no matter what community you were from.

A life-changing event for me was the murder of the three Scottish Soldiers. These were three young soldiers from Scotland who was lured away to what they thought was a safe location and killed.

People from within my community were telling me that it was the IRA who murdered them. I was led to believe that Roman Catholics were the IRA, as there was no evidence to say any other religion was part of that group.

As a child I never grew up saying to myself, someday I must kill a Catholic, but sometimes in life, we must use the deck of cards that has been set in front of us, that has been dealt to us, and with them, we can only decide how to play based on our knowledge at that time. Later, I would learn it was the Republicans[2] who were waging war against the Protestant community, but for now I had to protect our community. Our people were being murdered, so the Protestant communities established Loyalist[3] paramilitaries, who became the security forces. The reason for this was that the communities felt that

---
2 Republicanism became a violent movement for the unity and independence of Ireland under a republic.
3 Ulster loyalism emerged in the late 19th century, in response to the Irish Home Rule movement and the rise of Irish nationalism. This was where Protestants showed themselves to be more loyal to Britain.

the soldiers and police were not doing enough. There were terrorists out there and someone had to counter the terrorism. We were living on a knife edge with tension.

Within this setting, the paramilitaries, the local commanders, became my role models. I associated power with paramilitaries and respect. The paramilitary commander was the person who was going to keep our community together, defend it and fight the enemy. I wanted to be like that. I wanted to be respected. I saw it as the only way to defend my family and community.

I will share more in-depth later, but I joined the Ulster Defence Association[4] (UDA). I swore that I would do whatever was necessary to defend and defeat the IRA.

Well, that had been my vow, but I still did not expect the evening to turn out the way it did. I had gone out for a drink with my friends at a Loyalist Club. We'd had a few pints and then I headed for home and I was walking down the street, when I heard a familiar voice.

"Oso, have you got a gun?"

I turned and saw a group of men who were holding two Roman Catholic men against a wall. "No I don't, but I can get one," I replied.

As I was being asked that question, one of the men bolted and ran away. I told the others to go after the Catholic guy and get him, while I pulled the other Catholic guy into the entry to a building. I set myself up as judge, jury and executioner, and I took that young man's life on a cold January night in 1980. In that split second of killing him, I saw what all our family had gone through; how the Scottish soldiers had suffered and died, the pain that was inflicted, and in no more than a moment, it raged through me.

---

[4] At its peak of strength the UDA held around forty thousand members. In the '70s the Ulster Freedom Fighters were formed from the UDA with the focus on taking the war to the IRA more than on defence.

I'd be truthful if I said at the time that I was pleased with myself. I felt that I'd achieved something. I felt that maybe I had got one of those who had been killing people from my community. Years later, when I educated myself and I realised the seriousness of what I'd done, it actually scared the life right out of me. And I most certainly regretted the actions that I had taken on that night.

I think that what had happened to the Catholic men was that they had got into a taxi on North Street, and having found themselves in the wrong area, asked the taxi driver to take them to Ardoyne. Ardoyne was a Catholic area, but they would have had to travel through the Protestant area to get to the Ardoyne.

After the incident, I went to a friend's house and had a cup of tea; this really shows you the coldness of my heart. A mother would be told shortly that the son she had raised had been found murdered and here I was drinking tea. When I called into a local shop on the way home, a detective came in asking if there was anyone suspicious in the area. I remember standing in the shop with blood still on my shoes. I slid my feet under a rack. Everyone answered the same — no one had seen anything, including me. I then went back past the scene of the crime and stood with the RUC[5] and looked at the body. I remember having my name taken. Because the killing was not authorised by the local paramilitaries, I had to go to my local commander's house to explain what had happened.

It was the beginning of a sequence of events in my life and after that night it would cause me to be in and out of prison because I caused trouble with a capital T. I rebelled against authority, and yet here was I taking another person's life.

I am sure that the mother of that Catholic lad cried sore, just like the mother of a Protestant lad who would have been killed in revenge. No

---

5 The Royal Ulster Constabulary was the police force in Northern Ireland from 1922 to 2001. It was founded on 1 June 1922, as a successor to the Royal Irish Constabulary following the partition of Ireland. At its peak the force had around 8,500 officers, with a further 4,500 who were members of the RUC Reserve.

matter how we say it, or seek to justify it, no one wants to see the tears of a mother fall; there's something special about a mother.

***

I was a young lad, growing up amid violence. Surviving meant fighting; there was no other choice. Stand up for yourself, stand up for your brothers, or be trampled upon. That was it; that was life; I didn't know any other way.

My parents named me Alex Calderwood, otherwise widely known as Oso. I was born in 1962, and raised in a small community called Brown's Square, Shankill Road, Belfast. Our home was located on Sackville Street where there were between sixty to seventy houses. It was to become a concrete jungle, made famous because of the Troubles in Northern Ireland. My dad was called Thomas Calderwood, but he was known as Mousey. My mum was called Ellen, or Nellie as a friendship name. I didn't know what it was to have much, my family was poor. I am thankful for the parents that I had. I had four sisters and four brothers, although my brother Thomas died when he was young.

Young Oso

Sally was the eldest, followed by Elizabeth. Then it was Hugh John, who was known as Charlie because he had very curly hair like the actor Charlie Drake. The second son's name was similar, he was called John Hugh. Although he was called White Chief, as that was the name of a bread that he liked to eat. The next in line was me, Alex, otherwise known as Oso. The sixth child and third daughter, was Mary-Anne and then there was Alice. I'm not sure when our Thomas was born, but he lived on in our hearts.

We all had our nicknames as we grew up. When I was young, about four years old, there used to be an ice-cream man called Mr Oso and I used to run into the house screaming, "Oso" for some ice-cream money.

So, that's how I got my name, because they used to say here comes Oso again. I'm just glad that the ice-cream man wasn't called Mr Softie.

They loved me, my brothers and sisters. We had the love of our parents and they were fiercely protective. They did their best for us and put food on the table.

In our house, my mum and dad had the front bedroom, my three brothers had the middle bedroom and my uncle had the back bedroom. There was no room for the girls, so they actually stayed with my granny. She lived just across the street, so they were close by.

Mothers took pride in their homes, and fathers, if they worked, would leave for their nine-five jobs. Front doors were wedged with a stone to remain open, whether someone was in the home or not. No one bothered anyone, nobody stole anything and everyone looked out for each other. Early morning you lay in your bed and listened to all the women with their scrubbing brushes, as they competed to see who could make the best half-moon shine on their doorstep. They never showed that they were competing, but everyone knew they really were.

For most children of that era, Friday night was bathtime. And one thing about my mum was that she never cared what size you were or how dirty you were, it was, "You next. Into the bath." But they were not like the bathtubs that we have in our homes today, we had a tin bath. Those who got in first were roasted in hot water and those who had to wait until last were frozen with cold water. My four sisters would be bathed first, then my two brothers and then me. Yes, I was always last and so, of course, I had the honour of having the dirtiest water left for me. I think that many times I went in cleaner than I came out.

My father worked in the shipyard and at the weekend he went hunting with a man called Roy McKay. They caught lots of rabbits and hares, and brought them back to the house. Already, I was learning a lesson about survival. On several occasions, he would catch up to sixteen rabbits and my mum would either make soup or put them into pies.

We took what we needed for the family and left the rest outside the front door on the footpath, for any of the neighbours who needed them. So, everybody looked after each other in those days. Your front door was always left open, you could walk into anybody's house at any time. As a wee treat when you were a child, you were given a big round of bread, spread with butter and sprinkled with sugar and topped with red or brown sauce. If you were lucky and got the heel of the bread, that was the best. We lived on rabbits, hares and fish in those days.

Oso's mum and dad

On a Sunday, we went to a place called Rockport, and got willicks, or winkles, as some people call them. They are a wee shell; a type of seafood that has a wee black eye in it. You boil them and then with the help of a pin, you prise them out of their shells. My dad used to get a bin to put the shells in, and he would have filled one to the brim on a Sunday. We used to boil them in a pot with salt and pepper to get out all the dirt. I remember putting the pin in them with my dad before we put them in jam jars with vinegar, and let them soak for a while. There was nothing so lovely as eating them with a round of bread and butter.

Because we didn't have a lot of money, our toys were all homemade by a family member or a friend in the community. One day, my dad told me that he was going to be making something that I would like.

Feelings of excitement and joy rose within me as I wondered what it was going to be. He found an old door and then removed the hinges and the door handle. Then he took an old pram apart and attached the wheels of it to the door. He was building what we called a guider. I could not wait until he was finished to show my mates my high-end luxury wagon; well in my eyes, that's what it was. If I wasn't playing with my guider, I would be playing games in the street.

My first memories of playing on the street was on Micky Marley's roundabout. He had a big cart, like a wee funfair with wee horses going round it. He brought it round on a horse and cart. I used to get on and have a ride on it. I always remember as a young person playing football on the streets. And we used to play *Cribby*. One person would stand on one side of the street and the other person would stand on the other side. You threw the ball and tried to hit the footpath. If you managed to hit the footpath, it went back out again and if it hit the curb, you got a point.

We also played *kick the tin,* where a tin can was kicked as far away as possible. One person would be nominated to find the tin and put it in the *den*. Everyone else would run away and hide. The person who was *on,* would then have to find everybody. When you were *caught,* you had to go to the den and wait until everybody had been found.

The person who was caught first would then be *on*. If anyone who was hiding, managed to make it to the den without being caught, they could *kick the tin* and the game would begin again. Arallyo was similar to *kick the tin*. You played in teams. You had to kick a tin and go and find people. If you were spotted and they got back before you and kicked the tin, then you were out and they won the game.

I remember going to Sunday School when I was seven years old. It was the Elim Pentecostal Church on Townsend Street. My Sunday School teacher was called Mrs Snowdon. She tried to teach children how to follow the right path. "You need to change your ways," she said to me. But thinking I knew better I went my own way. At that point in time, it was not for me and I was expelled from Sunday School for kicking her leg. Later on, when I became a Christian, Mrs Snowdon sent me a letter to say that she had continued to pray for me when I'd left Sunday School.

People told me I was stupid when I was growing up; they were people in the community. There was unemployment everywhere. No one was enthusiastic and everyone lived with a negative attitude. It was hardly surprising that I ended up getting into trouble; I had no prospects.

There was no one to encourage me, no one who understood that I found learning difficult. Rather than trying to help, it was easier to label me as stupid.

School was not a happy memory for me. I didn't have any friends, but I don't think that I wanted any. I remember my first day at primary school. I walked into my classroom and looked at my teacher. She was called Mrs Taylor and she must have been about six foot six; she scared the life out of me. I was frightened. Here were people in authority outside of family. They were strangers. I did not know any of the teachers, although the school was only three hundred yards from my house. I climbed underneath the big cupboard inside the door, because I did not want to be there.

As a child, I remember that someone gave me a hand up so that I could look in the window. Now, I can look straight in, but it isn't a school anymore, it's a government training scheme. I stayed in that primary school until I was eleven. It was difficult. Bullies called me names such as *Stupid* and *Doe Doe*. I was also slow at learning and this led to me messing about, to get away from the work. Because I couldn't understand what I was taught at school and I struggled to read and write, I looked elsewhere for entertainment and that meant getting into trouble.

I went to Somerdale Secondary School when I was eleven and I did not progress much. I got expelled at eleven and a half. One day, I was sitting in the class when one of the boys in the class broke the back of a wooden chair while the teacher was writing on the blackboard. The boy threw the block of wood at the teacher and it landed and struck the blackboard right beside the teacher's head. The teacher turned and saw me laughing. It was my nerves, which were making me laugh; it wasn't me who had thrown it. I genuinely had not done it. When he saw me laughing, the teacher assaulted me by slapping me on the head. And I thought, what?! So, I lifted a chair and hit the teacher over the head with it because I had been hit for something I hadn't done. Then the teacher came at me with everything he had, so I opened the window and climbed up, ready to jump out.

"If you hit me, I'm jumping," I said.

"Alex, calm down," he said.

"No, you calm down. If you hit me, then I'm jumping," I replied. The window was high up and I probably wouldn't have jumped, but he got my legs back in and walked me to the headmaster's office.

"Put your hand out," said the headmaster as soon as I was in his office.

He meant to cane me.

"Not a chance," I replied.

"Put your hand out," he repeated. But there was no way that I was giving him the satisfaction. So, he grabbed me by my head, put his arm around my neck and started smacking me on my head with the cane. He hit me about three or four times. And I tell you, it stings.

This caused me to fall against his desk. Then he turned on me.

"Get out of my school and never come back." He was fuming. So I never went back. I was put out of school and that was the end of my formal education for a number of years.

It was clear that education did not work for me. School and Oso did not mix, in fact, it just created a toxic situation. I struggled to learn; I didn't understand what I was taught. I found everything difficult.

Therefore, trouble led me down the wrong path. After being wrongly accused at secondary school, I found it impossible to yield to authority. I wasn't able to toe the line, as we say.

At just twelve years old, I got a job working in a bar called The Diamond Jubilee. The man who owned the pub was called William Milford, and the bar manager was called William McFadden. He practically ran the bar for the owner. I started off lifting glasses and bottles and washing glasses. Then I began working behind the bar pulling pints. Everybody knew me and I got to know everybody. We ran darts in the bar and had a Shankill football team. It was different company from younger people and I felt as though I fitted in. The adults who came in were dependent on drink and that is how they socialised. People think that Jason Statham was the original *Transporter* but I was doing it way before that film series was ever written. I knew all the managers and those of influence, if you know what I mean. Local pubs were; Galls (The Wee Bar), The Limelight, The Elk Inn, Salisbury, Windsor, The Long Bar, The Horse Shoe, The Royal Bar, The Bricklayers Arms, Lizzie Thompsons, The Berlin Arms (Previously known as The Greyhound).

One of UDA's shows of strength

The paramilitaries used to come in and I got to know them. Unbeknown to me it was the planning base for the notorious C-Company of the Ulster Defence Association (UDA). Parcels were dropped off and left behind the bar. I had people say to me, take this parcel here and take this parcel there. And as a cover, I just put a bag-pack on my back, so if I saw anybody, they wouldn't think it was suspicious. But then if I was realistic about it, I probably didn't understand the significance of what I was doing. I just thought that I was doing something that was a good turn for somebody. I was young; it was a natural part of life. I ended up running up and down the Shankill, going into all the bars whether it was UDA or UVF (Ulster Volunteer Force[6]). That's why I became a well-known character. I knew everybody individually and sometimes

---

6 The UVF was initially formed in 1913, as a resistance to Home Rule, and 24,600 rifles were imported. Later in 1965, there was a re-emerging of a newly formed UVF to combat Irish Republicanism.

it was like a gangster film. The air was filled with smoke and drink; people were alert yet relaxing; guns were on the move and plans were being made; even ladies of the night were coming and going. And they thought Hollywood wasn't true; as a young teen I found it exciting.

Gradually, I saw the need for our community to have their own security. After all, if the police and the soldiers had been doing their job, the fighting would have stopped. So, it would be up to those who I knew and others, including myself, to take the fight to the terrorists.

I did that for a couple of years and then I started helping out at a chip shop. I had got to know the family who ran it and the manager Hughie.

So, from the age of eleven and a half, up to fifteen, no one from the education authorities came anywhere near me. I was free of them.

Chapter 2
Troubled Times and the Three Soldiers

You could say that I was *a child of the Troubles* or *Here comes trouble*.

But for me, trouble was all around, yes, I seemed to be Trouble with a capital T. It was the environment that I grew up in, I was breathing, eating and sleeping it; there was no escape. It was as if I had been dropped into a pit with no way out.

I was just seven years old when the Troubles started. The streets of the Shankill Road, the heart of the conflict, was where I spent my childhood.

Riots, petrol bombs and gun battles became a part of everyday life as the opposing community waged war, and I grew accustomed to it.

In 1969, when the Troubles started, the army put up a barricade at the end of our street, Sackville Street, to segregate us from the next street which was a Catholic Street called Coaches Street. This was the focus of the rioting. To begin with, it was just barbed wire to split the two communities. After some time, it was changed to a big timber fence.

Between these two streets there was a large gable wall. With the intense battles and rioting, the soldiers from the barracks were unable to get round to the soldiers on the other side. Two of these soldiers used to sit on top of the wall so that they could keep watch. My mother and the women in the area made sandwiches and a flask of tea for the soldiers as they sat on top of the wall for long periods of time. They let a rope

down from the top of the wall and then mum would tie the rope on to her shopping bag with the sandwiches and a flask of tea inside and the solders pulled the bag up. My mum and the rest of the women fed these soldiers for six months. Sometime later, the soldiers presented these women with flowers for looking after them.
At that time, there was a real community spirit in the Shankill.

Everyone was concerned about each other; it was about protecting your community. Older children grew up quickly because they had to protect their wee brothers and sisters. There were many nights when I heard gun battles; it was very frightening. When the rioting started, there were petrol bombs and water cannons. What had been abnormal soon become normal for the residents — the unbearable smell of burnt houses, burnt-out cars, lorries and buses. Anything that amounted to a barricade was used at the bottom of our streets to create a form of security. And even for me, as young as I was, I wished I was older so I could protect my sisters and brothers — my family.

Brown's Square community was a small pocket at the very bottom of the Shankill Road. It was a working-class, isolated, Loyalist community.

During the early years, if there had been rioting in any part of the Shankill or Crumlin Road, then the people of the Shankill Road had to protect their communities. This meant that Brown Square was left vulnerable at the bottom of the Falls. When there was rioting, there did not seem to be any law or order — everyone ran about mad.

The streets were generally quiet during the day, it was darkness that brought out the sound of gun, bomb and beatings. Every night, full-scale riots took place between the community that I lived in — the Protestant Shankill versus the Catholic Falls. In areas the children would be piled into one bedroom, the house that was always the furthest away from the trouble. For example in Bilton Court, in one bedroom, there was one double bed, there were about twenty children. All the children were terrified because they didn't know what was going to happen, but the adults did their best to keep us safe. When they got up the next morning, glass, stones and bottles were scattered everywhere.

On the occasions when I didn't get rushed out of my house, I hid in the coal bunker; which was underneath the stairs. I could still hear all the gun battles and shooting. It was terrible. And when there were no riots, it was only a matter of waiting until I heard an explosion, a bomb going off, or tac, tac, tac, gunfire — someone was being murdered.

Little did I know, that in just a few years, I would become one of those players in the war.

There came a time, when it wasn't safe to stay in our house anymore.

One morning, at 2 a.m., we were sleeping in our beds, when suddenly, I became aware of Mum and Dad scurrying around, and pulling the children out of their beds. They lifted the younger ones into their arms and there was a lot of commotion with us crying. People on the streets were shouting as we were herded down the stairs and on to the street.

The riots had started to intensify and we needed to be taken to safety.

So, there we were, in the middle of the night, walking among exploding petrol bombs, in our bare feet. At that time, there was a small court, called Bilton Court, situated in the middle of Brown's Square. All the children, including us, were housed in these courts for safety because houses were being burnt out by Republicans. Children were locked in with their mothers who took care of them. The fathers, and the boys who were old enough, had to go back on to the streets to defend their homes from being burnt by the Republicans. For the next few years there was hand-to-hand fighting in the streets as the Republicans, many of whom were IRA members, invaded and burnt our homes, while in retaliation, the Protestants enacted the same revenge. It was two sides of the community attacking each other.

When I look back now, I see that the Troubles was a manifestation of people's hearts; injustice caused a reaction that led to mayhem and death. I'm not saying that was an excuse, but if you keep the water boiling on the old stove, then sometime soon it will blow the lid off the saucepan.

I understood about hate — I adopted it as my friend and it did the same with me — we hung out together. My hatred was bottled up anger, which led me on many occasions to stand in front of a judge for fighting and petty crime.

The old saying *Love is Blind*, I believe, should be redefined to *Hate is Blind*. Certainly, it was the case for me. I continued to disrupt the holidays for both Catholics and even Protestants.

We lived in Brown Square until 1971, in a house that had the thrills of an outside toilet that you didn't want to go to when the snow was on the ground, and a tin bath in which the watered boiled the skin if you were first in, or you were frozen and likely dirtier if you were the last. For the locals we would go the bath house which was a small building in Malvern Street that held six baths in it, and paying a small fee got one a bath.

When we moved to the Shankill Estate later in 1971, it was great because we had a garden at the front of the house, a garden at the back, and wait for it — an inside toilet and a bath. We never had bedrooms in those days and we were lucky if we had a blanket, which was tough in the wintertime. If we needed the toilet during the night, then we had to go outside, so that was best avoided. There was one house where they had a bath, and they charged two bob or five pence, to use it. Therefore, you can imagine our delight when we moved house.

Soldiers building a division between both communities, near Oso's home

In some areas of Belfast, it was the same as the time when the Germans bombed Belfast, but it wasn't Germans who were destroying the town — it was the town's own people. Then the British Army arrived to try to instil order and control the fighting.

Then one day out of nowhere, a sound erupted down the street. I did not know what it was until I saw these massive armoured personal carriers roaring through minor barricades before they screeched to a stop. Soldiers in camouflage uniform jumped out with their SLRs (self-loading rifles) and hard hats. In their English accents, they shouted orders. "You over there, stand against the wall." Once they had secured the area, they erected their own barricades, which were mainly barbed wire. With the British Army standing between the Catholic and Protestant communities, for a few weeks, quiet returned to the areas.

Then it erupted again with riots, but an extra community was involved with a new weapon — CS gas. Soldiers shot CS gas as if they were passing out smarties to children. To prevent the CS gas from entering our homes, people replaced the curtains with blankets, which they drenched in water and hung over the inside of their windows. Surely, this was not a normal life for any child?

I could write about the time when the soldiers hurt the Protestant communities as much as the Catholic communities, but we should never forget that they came into the middle of two waring communities, to keep the peace and they helped a lot of adults to safety. Anyone who had a Northern Irish accent, even if they were serving the soldiers tea, could have been the very person to set them up to be murdered the next day, especially when the Catholic communities turned on them.

The Royal Highland Fusiliers regiment in whom the Scottish soldiers belong to was stationed in Girwood Barracks and based in Brown Square. When I was nine years old, I became the British Army's mascot in Brown Square Barracks for them. I had my own wee uniform and my own wee bed in the room inside their barracks. I used to make tea and toast for the soldiers who were on the sanger,[7] who were guarding the barracks. I used to go to the shops and get them chocolate, cigarettes and lemonade. The soldiers would give me loaves of bread, cheese, cooked ham and other meats. The reason for this was, I would bring the food to my mum and other women and in turn they would make sandwiches for the soldiers on patrol.

I looked up to these Scottish soldiers; they were kind to me and became my friends. I got to know them that well, that when it was my birthday,

---

7 A temporary fortified position with a breastwork originally constructed of stones, and these days built of sandbags, concrete, gabions or similar materials.

they took me to Woolworths in North Street and bought me a toy self-loading rifle (SLR). When I went back to the barracks, I must have been messing too much with the rifle because it broke.

They took me back to the shop because I was crying and bought me a new one. Having a toy was so cool and whenever their captain was not around, they used to let me sit in the back of their Land Rover.

They drove me around my own area where I'd sit with my toy SLR as I looked out of the back with a soldier sitting opposite me — his SLR was real. I must admit that for safety reasons, they never took me any further than my own street. I have plenty of good memories of my time with the Scottish soldiers.

These soldiers had come in to try to help people live together, and the next minute they were being attacked. In 1971, I remember the news filtering through our community that the three Scottish Soldiers were found murdered in Ligoniel, North Belfast. It happened on March 10, when the Provisional Irish Republican Army shot dead three, unarmed British Army soldiers of the 1st Battalion, Royal Highland Fusiliers. Two of the three soldiers were teenage brothers, John (17) and Joseph McCaig (18); and the other one was Dougald McCaughey (23); all three were from Scotland.

The three Scottish soldiers had fallen into what was believed at the time, a honeytrap that lead them to their deaths. This was a trap used by Republican women, who would either be members of the IRA or IRA sympathisers. They enticed their target into a so-called, one-night stand and invited them to an agreed address. The target would not realise that they were being watched at a distance while all of this was taking place. Then at the appropriate time, IRA terrorists entered, the women left and the target was executed on the spot or taken away to be executed.

These three young soldiers had been granted an afternoon pass that allowed them to leave their base. McCaughey's younger brother was serving in the same unit but was on duty and unable to join them.

They were off-duty, unarmed and in civilian clothes. They were drinking in Mooney's, a Belfast city centre pub in Cornmarket, one of the safer areas of the city for soldiers at this stage of the conflict. One report said that the three soldiers were lured into a car by Republican women. But history would tell us that it was a man with an English voice, an ex-paratrooper[8], who promised them a party where women would be at. The three were taken to the White Brae, Squire's Hill, off the Ligoniel Road in north Belfast. There they were shot dead by Provisional IRA members; two of them in the back of the head and the other in the chest.

The Three Scottish soldiers

John McCaig (age 17)
Dougald McCaughey (age 23)
Joseph McCaig (18)

---

8 Paddy O'Kane served as a paratrooper in the British army from 1957-1964. His fingerprint was also found on the Kingsmill bus massacre. He obtained On The Run letter from the British government.

At the inquest in 1971, it was established that all three were shot at very close range, probably as they stood in a line. The jury was told that the three were probably shot while relieving themselves beside the road. "You may think that this was not only murder, but one of the vilest crimes ever heard of in living memory," said the coroner. The bodies were heaped on top of each other and two beer glasses were lying nearby. Their bodies were found by children at 9:30 p.m.

Even though I did not know these young lads personally, their murder had a big impact on me. Only days earlier, I was having fun with one of the soldiers from the same unit and then the next thing I knew, they had been found murdered. I had permission from my parents to travel to Dundee in Scotland with him. I didn't go to the funeral though as I was only nine years old at the time, so I stayed with the soldier's mother. This event had a profound effect on me and stayed with me for the rest of my life. The question I asked myself at that time was who killed the three Scottish soldiers?

I learnt that it was not a normal society when people carried guns. The community of Brown Square completely changed with the Troubles.

Sackville Street, and my street was demolished. Very rarely did I leave my area. The city centre was unsafe.

Chapter 3

Sleeping with your Enemy

I opened my eyes and looked around. The lights were high above my head. I heard voices. I turned my head to the side. I saw a bed. I turned my head the other way. There was another bed. I realised that I was lying on a bed. I wanted to rub my eyes, but I couldn't move my arm. Was this a dream? Where was I? I tried to get up, but I couldn't. I looked down. I was strapped to the bed. How did I get there? I looked at the other beds. Was I in a hospital? If I was on a ward in a hospital, then why were these beds screwed to the floor? My head felt fuzzy and I had begun to drift off to sleep when I heard voices again and they were getting nearer. Only, I couldn't make out what they were saying, yet they were walking towards me. It was then I realised that they were speaking another language.

Two nurses stared down at me. They muttered something to each other and then one of them pulled up my sleeve. I felt something wet on my arm and suddenly it was painful. The nurse had given me an injection. The dull ache in my arm reminded me that this hadn't been the first injection. As I drifted off into another delirious form of sleep, my memory slowly returned.

I woke to a plate of food. I was allowed to sit up and eat, although I was still restrained. It reminded me of a prison. No one spoke English, so I was restrained mentally and physically. I figured out that everyone was speaking Dutch, but I did not realise that I was in a mental hospital.

Even though I didn't understand why I was there, I began to remember what had happened earlier.

It was 1976, and I had been sent on a community holiday to Holland.

The community leaders thought that it would be great to create cross-community outreaches with the intention of integrating both sides of the community. They gathered a group of about twenty Catholics and twenty Protestants. It was the first time that I had come into contact with *the other side* since the beginning of the Troubles in 1969. What was meant to be a holiday, turned out to be a holiday from hell, and this was before the television programme had been thought about.

We arrived at the airport, had a look at the shops and then headed towards the escalator. Already, there was tension in the air. You could feel it from both sides as we looked each other up and down and hisses came from inside the chests of each group. The clock was ticking; it was only a matter of when. Whoever thought that this was a good idea must have had their head in the clouds. As we were going up the escalator, one of the Catholic guys looked at me in a way that I did not appreciate. I did not waste any time. I grabbed hold of his shoulders, headbutted him and he rolled the whole way down the escalator onto the floor. Mayhem broke out at the airport. I was fourteen years old with a lot of hatred in my heart because of the way I had grown up. I was upset about the incident with the three Scottish soldiers. I was angry that people were being murdered in my community. The perception that I had at this time was that it was them or us. Here was the Catholic community who had wreaked so much havoc in my Protestant community, and they were expecting us to go away together? Did they really think that they were going to bring peace and reconciliation on a holiday trip to Holland? The problem was that this group who had organised the holiday, had paid for it and were committed to go on it. My thoughts were that although we were going away together, we were not going to get on. I saw every one of them as the enemy, be they male or female.

As we got on the plane, everyone became mixed up. There was very little chat; everyone was on a knife edge. This was the first time that I had been on a plane and I was nervous. Once we were in the air, the pilot asked each of us to take it in turns to look through the windows in the cockpit. This interested me, but when I walked up and saw the clouds, it scared the life out of me. I felt frightened because I realised that I was afraid of heights. All I could see were the clouds and they looked like sponges or pieces of snow and I could not understand how I was high up above this.

When we landed, everyone was split up. One Protestant and one Catholic were designated to each house. This was their method of cross community. Unbelievably, I was put in the same house as the lad who I had been fighting with in the airport; not a good decision.

How do you sleep in a room with your enemy, especially one that you've just headbutted? The house was nice, and the Pilgrim's family were welcoming. These kind people had brought us in to be a part of their family, but unfortunately, I did not appreciate that at the time.

Everything that they seemed to eat was with cheese, but it was good.

They gave us as much food as we wanted to eat. Then, they showed us to our room, but we did not get on. I had it in my head that I was going to fix this Catholic boy's waggon. In other words, I was going to pick a fight with him. I beat him over the head with a shoe. He did not take kindly to this and told our Pilgrim carers. They isolated me in a room before I was removed from the house and taken away.

I was put in the house with the leaders so that they could keep an eye on me and I got a room on my own which I was happy about. There were some occasions when I was allowed to be with the group, but I was not allowed to participate in any activities. Everyone else had opportunities to do things, but I was kept on my own. After the first week, they decided to isolate me from the group altogether as I was causing trouble. Everyone else was getting on with each other except me. Then they put me with a big paratrooper, an ex-soldier to look after me. This guy was like a policeman, and he took me out for a walk.

But I did not want to stay with him, so any opportunity I got, I ran away. Late one night at about 2 a.m., I pulled a prank. I took all the leader's shoes and filled them with mud. They really did not appreciate it, no matter how much I tried to convince them to smile. The leaders had had all they could take of me. So, the people in charge decided to send me away, and the next thing I knew I was in this strange room. I was strapped on to a bed and curtains were pulled round. They started giving me injections; apparently, they were to knock me out and calm me down. But they sent me into a weird delirium. After three days, I woke up on the ward. At the bottom of the ward there were small rooms with beds in the middle and there was special glass. I remember all this.

I also remember this guy with a big beard. He sat outside my room and waved at me. After a few days, they allowed me out of the room to mingle with the others. I did not know where I was or who the people around me were. I remember walking along the ward. Halfway down the ward, was a metal grill, but it was locked with a key. I asked if I could go into the TV room. They let me in, but the television was in Dutch, so that was no good to me. All I can recollect is a wee chap who used to sit beside his bed playing a guitar, and I suppose that was something I could identify with. So, I used to sit on his bed and listen to him playing his guitar. He gave me a T-shirt as a gift. This man seemingly cared about me and we bonded. I remember him showing me kindness and giving me something. The family I was supposed to be staying with brought me clogs and a present. These people still made an effort. Then they came and collected me and took me back to the airport.

Oso in his early teens

The way the people in charge responded was to send me to a mental hospital. There was no one there who could speak English, only Dutch.

I was there for three weeks. So, basically, I was left alone in this place.

I was fourteen years of age and incarcerated with a lot of adults who were strangers. I was not allowed back with the group at all. They even sent me home on a separate plane. It was such a strange flight. because I felt like an outsider isolated from my previous travelling companions.

This should never have happened. I should never have been sent to that hospital alone. It was a very hurtful experience. I thought I was never going to get home. I had to tell my parents what I had been through.

My dad became angry. I remember there were all sorts of arguments, but I was back with my own people.

Of course, it affected my mental health. My dad hit the youth leader for doing that to me. Sometime after the holiday, they decided to have a sponsored disco so that they could get together again. I decided to go and I danced at the disco for hours and hours.

Because of all my problems that were causing me to miss school, my mum took me to see a psychiatrist on Lincoln Avenue, just off the Antrim Road. I was fourteen at the time. However, I don't know why, but I did not get on with him. A lot of different assessments were carried out on me, but I didn't understand what they were because nothing was explained to me. After he had assessed me, he said that *he* needed to see a psychiatrist.

I was then taken down to Rathgael Training School which was a children's home for boys with troubled backgrounds. I was told that I was being sent there because I hadn't been attending school and refused to be educated. When I arrived, the other boys were having a meal so I sat down to eat with them. I told the headteacher that I was going to go home as soon as I'd eaten. He did not take kindly to that and said that I would need to stay otherwise he would contact the police.

However, I told him that he could ring the police if he wanted to, but I did not want to stay there, so I left as soon as I'd had my dinner.

I did not hear anymore until I was fifteen. Then the education officials came and said that they were going to have to do something with me.

They decided to send me to Fallowfield Boarding School. At that time we had a family member from New Zealand staying with us, so they were able to take me in a car to the boarding school.

When I arrived, I was taken into the headmaster's office. My suitcase full of clothes was taken from me
"Have you got any cigarettes on you?" asked the headmaster.

"Yes I do," I replied. He told me to give him my cigarettes. So I gave him a packet without telling him that I had kept one packet. This happened early in the morning. I was then taken into the classroom at about 9 a.m. I sat there with all the other kids. We had a break at 9:45 a.m. They gave us some milk and then I went outside, lit a cigarette and started smoking.

"What do you think you're doing?" said one of the teachers who came up to me.

"What do you think I'm doing? I'm having a smoke," I replied.

"You're not allowed to smoke."

"Well, who's going to stop me?"

"I'm going to stop you."

"No, you're not."

He took me back to the headmaster's office. "Give me your cigarettes," said the headmaster.

"No, I'm not giving you my cigarettes."

So, he took me in his car to the train station and put me on a train back home to Belfast. When I got to Belfast, I walked inside the house and saw my dad sitting in the living room. He looked surprised.

"What are you doing back?" he asked me. I told him that they'd thrown me out. He couldn't believe it.

"What?" he said.

I told him again. "They threw me out." My ma hadn't got back yet, so I hid behind the chair in the living room. When she and my uncle arrived, I heard her say, "Thank God, that's Alex out of the way." So, I jumped up from behind the settee.

"Hey Ma, that's not very nice."

She was taken aback. "What are you doing here?" she asked. That's exactly how it happened. So, consequently that was the end of boarding school.

Just when I thought that I had escaped from the education system, the authorities had not forgotten their duty. They sent a remedial teacher to the house. I told her that I did not want to learn, that there was no point because I just drank wine and beer all the time. But she was unrelenting and said that I would have to come up with a compromise.

I thought on my feet. "I'll tell you what the compromise will be. If you can take me up to the baths and let me go for a swim, then I'll let you teach me," I replied. She agreed, and the next week when she collected me, she took me for a swim. I think that deep down, she had a soft spot for me. So, that was my education, just one hour each day with a personal tutor. But it didn't last long, and I still hadn't learnt how to read and write.

Chapter 4
Paramilitaries Became My Family

When I look back on my life and reflect, and wonder why some of the things that happened, actually took place, I wonder at the impact that it had. You see, if every event that I was involved in was listed in this book, well it would be a very large book. However, if you were to consider every event as a *kicking* of my mind and body, then we would likely agree, that as a human being it would be difficult to walk upright. So, it was for the many young men and women who lived in areas of the war zone. What choice did they have but to deal as best as they could with the cards that had been dealt to them. For those of us who were one-time young in this field, no one could know what the outcome was going to be, or the full consequences of what would unfold. We based our decisions on what we knew at the time. And I think, if it had been different, how would I have turned out. But then, I know with everything I've been through, God still gives us a choice, and for us who like to know for sure what the answer is … God says … choose life.

When I was fifteen, something happened in front of me that is hard to make sense of, something that epitomised, not just the horror of the Troubles, but the craziness of it as well.

I used to play a game called the *pitch and toss*. You used a stick of wood that was about five inches (12cms) long and you put two ha'pennies on the stick. Then you threw them above your head. Your friends would take bets on whether they would land on two heads or two tails. If it fell on two heads, and you had backed the heads then you were the winner. The *banker* made his money by getting people to bet on the best of three games. To win money, you had to have three wins in a row.

Meaning, three sets of heads shown upright on the coin when it landed. I was with my friends, and I had made a few pounds, so we went for a drink in the Shankill. We were sitting there drinking and chatting, and minding our own business. There was a wee back room and a wee front room in this pub, and we were sitting in the back room when out of nowhere we heard … bang, bang, bang, bang. Shots were being fired.

I leant back on my chair and I saw this guy lying in the passageway, so I retreated.

"Somebody has just been shot, what do I do?" I asked my two friends.

"Don't do nothing, just keep on drinking," they replied nervously. I kept on drinking and then the people who ran the bar came over to us.

"Somebody's just been shot so take your drinks and go around to another club as the police is on their way. So, we lifted our drinks and went to another club, set our glasses on the table and continued to drink.

When I reflect back on that moment, I think what a terrible state of affairs it was. Someone had just been murdered and we were expected to continue drinking?! There was a sense that as we were young, we were immune to it and we didn't know how to react. When something happens that is so far removed from the *norms* of society, there is no code or rulebook that outlines how to behave. In those kinds of bizarre circumstances, because you are thrown into shock and don't have an idea of what to do, the tendency is just to carry on as normal. But it was not normal, it really was not normal. But unfortunately, that was the way it was at the time. Someone had just had an argument with a guy and this was his way of settling the argument, by shooting him.

I remember drinking my first pint when I was sixteen with my father in the Diamond Jubilee. To me this was one of the aspects of becoming a man. My dad had taken me to the pub and bought his son his first pint; it made me feel important. That moment when your dad says, "Here son, I'm going to buy you a pint." It was as if all the hairs on my chest had grown at once. I felt that in one sentence my dad had said, "You're now a man." It forced the people in the bar to look at me in a different light and it gave me a sense of belonging. I had two older brothers and they had been accepted in the crowd; I wanted that too.

When I looked around, the paramilitaries were the in-crowd that I wanted to belong to. As a man, I had to make decisions. I had to decide on whether I was going to join the Ulster Volunteer Force (UVF) or the Ulster Defence Association (UDA). After all, the Troubles were not going away and my community needed protecting. When I looked back to my childhood, I remembered being herded out of the house in the middle of the night and put into Bilton Court for protection. When I reflected on that time, I realised that it was the sixteen and seventeen year olds who were protecting me. These were the ones who led the younger children to safety. Although we had moved to the Shankill Estate, I wanted to be someone who could protect my community. They were protecting the kids of their area and now I wanted to do the same.

A UDA unit in training, early 70's

During the early seventies there was a sense of power in paramilitarism; it seemed exciting. When I saw that a lot of my mates were joining the Junior UDA, I decided it was time that I did as well. The identification was a wee blue jacket with a fur collar; I thought I was the bee's knees.

In a sense, joining the paramilitaries was like becoming part of one big family. The sense of belonging was so real, it made me feel invincible.

For many people, this was their only family. To become one of them, gave me an opportunity. It made me feel like a big lad, if you could look after someone younger than you.

I always believed that the paramilitaries were the protectors of our community. They were there to try and protect the younger people and I couldn't wait until I was older. The Junior UDA, called Ulster Young Militants, existed for sixteen and seventeen year olds because they didn't want you until you were eighteen.

So, at sixteen, I joined the Ulster Young Militants, and to join I had to be sworn in. I arrived at a predetermined location and was escorted into a room by men wearing balaclavas. When I entered the room, a table was in the middle of the floor. It was covered with an Ulster[9] flag[10]. On top of the flag sat a Bible and a gun. I was surrounded by men dressed in paramilitary uniforms, one on each side of me, and three sitting behind the table where they were gathered as witnesses to what I was about to agree too. I was always quite tough, but standing in that room on that day was like a shine was being given to my toughness.

The man in the centre of the table read out a statement and confirmed that I was agreeing to sign up as a volunteer of the UDA. I confirmed that I understood, and there I was — an official member of the UDA.

At that time, it was probably one of the most important steps in my life. Here I was, just a young person who'd grown up with no education.

I had gained life experience, working in a bar, but this would give me a sense of responsibility, a grounding. I was a mature young person, but I did have a weakness; I simply could not get my head around arguments and this led me into trouble.

People saw me differently in the bar when I became a member of the UDA. I was not simply the person who lifted the glasses, bottles and served the pints. I was the protector of that community. It made me feel good.

Each week we were given commands about what to do and where to be.

As in any army, orders had to be accepted without question. The first order I received was to turn up on one of the side streets, Greenland Street, for training. We were drilled on how to march properly and how to stand to attention. It was based on a military regime. We believed that

---
9 Ulster consisted of the most northern nine counties on the island of Ireland. Loyalists would hold true to the name Ulster even after partition.
10 Loyalists would call the Northern Ireland flag, the Ulster flag.

we were boy soldiers. There was also weapons' training and I was excited as a sixteen-year-old when I learnt how to use a gun. It was comfortable to know that there were guns there to protect the community. The war was against the Republican community; this was my perception at the time. I was led to believe that it was IRA Republicans who were trying to destroy our community. However, I was not an active member yet, and I had to go through an initiation period. My role at the beginning was to be there with my mates and give them moral support. I believed in what I was doing and I believed that I would make a difference. I wanted to be a man to protect others. As part of the community protection, I carried a gun from sixteen years of age and wherever I went, it went with me. It gave me authority because I knew that no one would give me orders. The gun also gave me a sense of power. Although I was still a kid, I was protecting my community.

Sadly, there are a lot of people who are now dead. People I had known in the young UDA. There were also people who moved out of the country. Often, later in life, people learn lessons and move on. There was one person I knew who understood that fighting back with weapons was not the answer. That person was my cousin, Jackie McKee; he was different.

Like me he had the same choice whether to join the paramilitaries or choose another path. Thank God, he picked Bible college and went to be trained in pastoring. It gave me a sense of pride. Here was my big cousin, who studied hard and joined the local church. Looking back, I should have taken heed of my cousin's life choices, but a hard head is difficult to get through to. Jackie's role model was Jesus Christ, but my role models were the people who directed killings and so forth. I think that this was because it was an easier way to justify my existence as a rebel against authority and especially against those who sought to kill my friends and family. I always wanted to join the army, and hanging out with soldiers meant that I felt as if I was part of them and I was where I belonged. The only thing that stopped me from joining the army was the fact that I could not read or write.

As you know now, when I joined the UDA there was no writing or reading test; it was more about doing. So, I felt like I'd started on a journey that I did not have control of, but I believed that this was my destiny. I had been programmed by my society and peers — what were this generation teaching their children? At the time, this seemed to be a natural course for any young man in the community. If you did not follow this road, it meant that you were a coward and that you did not want to be a part of the community. The paramilitaries were the community. They were the people who held the community together, simply because they protected it.

One day my mum sent me to the shop for a pint of milk and half a pound of butter. While I was out, I bumped into a friend who had come in to some money. We got talking and decided to take a trip to Scotland together. I went home and told my mum that I was going away for a while. I had a cousin who lived in the town of Kilwinning, so we went to stay with his family. My friend just stayed for a couple of weeks, but I ended up staying for a full year. I came home again to Belfast when I was sixteen.

I became good at stealing cars for operations and majority of obtaining these cars were successful except for one occasion. I was driving a stolen car and crashed it into a sign post, a set of traffic lights, and a telephone communications' box; they were all demolished. One of the other people in the car had to be cut out as some of his bones were broken and he had some fingers missing.

It was a Wednesday night, and there was a do[11] on with music in a Loyalist club. I went with my two friends who I hadn't seen in a year. We'd had a few drinks and then as we were leaving, my two friends got into a fight with this other guy.

On the Friday, I was sent for; I had to go to the UDA Headquarters in the Shankill. I was brought into a room and the staff[12] of the UDA

---
11 Local slang regarding an event.
12 Senior leaders.

were sitting around a table. "Oso, were you at the Loyalist club on Wednesday night?" one of them asked. I told them that I was, but that it had nothing to do with me. A man sitting at the table starred at me with an evil look and in a coldness, "Shoot him anyway," he said.

At the meeting, they decided that because this guy had been beaten up by my friends, the three of us were going to get kneecapped, in other words shot in the knee as punishment.

I suppose it is important for those of you who have never lived in a community ruled by paramilitaries to know that when they ask you to turn up, it's not a request, it is a command. And like any command from senior army ranks if it is not obeyed, the punishment is extreme.

So the best advice for me at that moment was to turn up and bring a towel to wrap around whatever part they decided to shoot.

I was told to go to a certain bar at lunchtime. Only two of us turned up though, the other guy did not. You need to imagine this. Me and my mate were in the bar; he had a towel in a plastic bag and I had one too.

When the time came, we were told to go into the alley, which we did.

At the bottom of the alley was a car with a man in it. He was the lookout for police or the authorities. His job was … if he saw anything suspicious or anyone who looked like a policeman, he was to toot the car horn.

As we were standing there a man with the gun came out of the pub.

"Shoot me first," I said. I just wanted to get it over with.

He took aim and I saw his finger squeeze the trigger. I closed my eyes and held my breath … instead of hearing shots I heard *toot, toot*.

The gunman put the gun into his coat and told us to wait there while he went back into the pub. We stood still; I am unsure for how long, but it was definitely for a while, then he reappeared, pulled out the gun and shot me in the leg. No warning was given.

He then shot my mate and stupidly, believe this, I should repeat this word, stupidly, I spoke up. "I think you've missed me," I said.

"What?" he replied in disbelief.

"I think you've missed me," I repeated. As he came over to shoot me again, it was then that I saw a trickle of blood running down my leg.

He had got me. I raised my hand. "It's okay, you got me, look …"

I shouted as I showed him the blood trickling down my leg. I knew that it had to be done because that was the way they did things. This was happening to a lot of people, but it could have been worse. I could have been shot dead. I guess you could say that we were getting off lightly. Then a police car drove past and shouted at us. "You guys okay?" the policeman called out. "Sure," we replied as we tried to keep our faces straight, and not show any pain and allow the wall to hold us up — that was life.

The Battle of Oriel Park, Dundalk …
I remember in 1979, when the battle of Oriel Park took place. Our local Belfast football team, Linfield, winners of the Irish League, who were mainly supported by Protestants were playing football against Dundalk football team, who were champions of the League of Ireland.

The match was to be played Dundalk, in the Republic of Ireland.

Dundalk's supporters were Catholic and Republican. Trouble was in the air.

Linfield's manager, Roy Coyle, was warned to keep their 5,000 strong supporters in check. Garda[13] was on high alert with all leave cancelled for the game. The night before the game, Linfield supporters were bussed across the border and into hotels in Dundalk.

Before the match whistle blew, the rioting started — stones, bottles and anything that could be found were thrown. The changing rooms were turned into a field hospital and rioters and policemen were carried into them.

Garda removing a rioter from the grounds

As the riot continued, the order came to take down the tri-colour flag.[14] I went for it, climbed up a pole onto the roof before I ran to the flag pole. Garda officers ran towards me knowing if that flag came down, there would be a higher level of rioting, while I knew, if the flag came down, it showed defeat to the Republicans. I started to kick the pole, pull the pole, push the pole until it started to come down. Suddenly a steward grabbed me. I punched him full in the face. He slid across the top of the roof. His coat caught on the edge of it. It was the only thing holding him forty feet in the air. As he hung there the Garda

---

13 The Republic of Ireland has one national civilian police force, called An Garda Síochána.
14 The national flag of Republic of Ireland and used by Republican groups for their funerals, draped over their volunteer coffin.

split into two sections, one section faced me and the other sought to save the steward's life.

They surrounded me, so I grabbed on to a pole at the side of the building and slid down. When I reached the bottom, the Garda just snatched me then they thumped, kicked and beat me. They covered me with their shields to stop missiles hitting them or me for that matter. I was escorted through the mass of angry people.

I was taken to the Garda station and placed into a cell with ten Dundalk supporters. Immediately, I knew I was in danger. One of the Dundalk men said, "He's a Linfield man, let's beat the crap out of him." But one of the other Dundalk men said, "We're going to need him when the guards come in."

Knowing I had to protect now myself from these Dundalk supporters and the guards when they would enter to beat up the prisoners, I thought I would pull a move. I started to bang the cell door until a guard came and then I asked, "could I use the toilet?" As soon as entered the hall — BANG, he punched me as hard as he could on my nose, breaking it and blood was now pouring from it.

The guy who went in before me received eighteen months which made me nervous. I think it was because I was only seventeen that I got away with a one hundred pound fine. They released me, and my mum and my mum's friend Annie Morrison came to collect me from Dundalk Station. I was relieved to be going back home on the train. No matter what I had done or what trouble I got myself into, my mum proved time and again, that she was always there for me.

Chapter 5
Hydebank Youth Prison

I had narrowly missed imprisonment for the incident in Dundalk. But it wasn't long before I found myself in trouble again. In 1980, I was sentenced to one year in the Young Offender's Centre at Hydebank.

I had been ordered to carry out a robbery in Reid's Shoe Shop on the Shankill, by the organisation that I had joined. The paramilitaries taxed their local shops and called it protection money. It was, in fact, extortion but most shop owners were happy paying ten or twenty pounds if it meant that they were protected and it kept everyone happy. However, if they didn't pay, then there would be a penalty as Reid's Shoe Shop found out.

We were told to clean the shop out, but it didn't quite go to plan.

There was an old man who lived next door to my friend who owned a van. The plan was to get him drunk and then steal his van. So, we brought a case of beer and gave it to my two associates. They were to go into his house and sit with the guy who owned the van and keep him occupied while we took the van and left my associates and the van owner alone together drinking the beer. We managed to do two or three runs to the shop, taking three to five thousand pounds worth of shoes. Meanwhile, while I was busy transporting, my associates had got themselves drunk on the case of beer. Forgetting why they were there, they walked home. The owner of the van came to his senses and realised that his van had been stolen. He phoned the police and told them everything. The police came quickly and caught us.

On the very first day at the YOC, you were expected to make all your sheets nice and square and neat. It was called a bed-pack. I was not used to dealing with sheets and making beds, so I just left them. "What's that on your bed? Are you trying to make fun of me?" said the prison officer when he came to inspect the bed making. Then he slapped me on my head and dragged me back into the cell. All I could see on the bed were the sheets and the blankets. "So, you think you're funny?" he said. And he slapped me again. "You see that, that's a bed-pack, I want you to make a bed-pack," he added. I couldn't cope with this guy telling me what to do and I lost my temper. I lifted the sheets and the blankets off the bed. "You see that, I'm not making it," I said. As a result, I got taken to the *boards,* otherwise known as the punishment cells, where I was locked up for twenty-three hours a day. All I was given was one hour's exercise a day. My blankets were taken out at eight in the morning and not returned until eight at night. I still got three meals a day, and after supper at eight, they gave me back my blankets.

I was left to sit there all day, with just a pot, a loo roll and a Bible. I could use the other two, but I could not read the Bible. For six months I was locked up for twenty-three hours per day.

When the UDA heard that I had been locked up on the *boards* for that long, they sent two UDA commanders to visit me. When they arrived, the No. 1 Governor came down with tea and coffee and tried to talk to my visitors. I didn't appreciate this as I only got one visit a month, so I told him to clear off. I certainly didn't want him interrupting my visit.

Later that night, a couple of prison officers were beaten up in the YOC car park. The next thing I knew, the governor was giving me tobacco, chocolate and sweets. "Now you need to speak to your friends, because I don't want any more of my prison officers beaten up," he said. "I don't know what you're talking about. It's nothing to do with me and it's nothing to do with my visitors," I replied, but he wouldn't accept that. "It certainly has to do with you and it certainly has to do with your visitors," he replied. "I don't know what you're talking about, it has nothing to do with me," I said. I was put back into the communal wing after six months in the *boards*.

Oso being interviewed on behalf of the UDA.

When I went into the wing, I was put in a cell with a Catholic lad from the Unity flats. He was called Richard or Dicky, as we knew him.

I had fought with Dicky on the outside. His flat was opposite where I lived on the Shankill Estate. There was only waste ground separating us. I used to go over and break the windows in the Unity flats and he would come over and break the windows in my area. My initial reaction was to headbutt him and get it over with. I had been locked up for twenty-three hours a day, I did not want to go back to that so I waited to see what he had to say. I told Dicky that I was not going to make a bed-pack, as I had been ordered to on the first day I had arrived, and that I had hit the prison officer with the sheets because I could not make it. Dicky surprised me by saying that we could work together. By this he meant that we would run the wings. "You be in charge of the Protestants and look after them, and I'll be in charge of the Catholics. Everyone will do what we tell them," he said. So Dicky made my bed-pack for me and we struck up a friendship. Together, we took control of the wing in Hydebank. If there was a Protestant problem, then I dealt with it and if it was a Catholic problem, then Dicky sorted it out. We became like brothers as we looked after each other and as a consequence my perception of ordinary Catholics changed.

I eventually got out in February, after having to serve an extra month because I hit an officer over the head with a brush. We had been watching television and I had changed the channel. Then the officer got up and changed the channel. "If anyone gets up and turns the TV over, then they'll get put on a charge," he said. I was not happy, so I got up and changed it. "If anyone turns that TV over then they'll pay for it," I said. He was having none of it, and he got up and changed it again. So, I got up, lifted a brush and hit him. Then the alarm went off and I was sent back to the *boards*.

At this point in my life, Christianity was something I had not thought about. When I was in the YOC there were people trying to get me into Bible studies, but remember I could not read or write properly. The only person I ever thought about was Jackie McKee. He was part of my family and as I have already said, he was a Christian. I knew that my mother and father loved me, but they were both opposed to violence.

But my whole mind was in turmoil because I had taken someone's life and I realised that my friends were in prison because of something that I had done. I suppose it did have a psychological effect on me. I didn't know what was happening to me, but I felt sorry for my mates and I felt sorry for myself. During all that confusion, I didn't have anyone to talk to about it. I couldn't make sense of the thoughts inside my head, and I wondered if they came from God. There were so many of my friends and so many people that I knew, who were dead. And I didn't really want to keep going down that road.

My friends who had been convicted for the murder, weren't even there when it took place. Their convictions came because they were interrogated in Castlereagh Holding Centre. The police must have been after a certain number of convictions that month, as they refused to let them go and forced them to admit to being there. It should have been me. I saw the people who were holding the two Catholic men. I thought that they were going to kill the other man who had ran off and so that's why I killed the guy who I took into the entry. I said when they came back after chasing the other man. "Where's the other guy?" "He's dead," they said. "He's what? Did you shoot him?" I replied. Then there was pandemonium as they panicked. They didn't catch the other guy; he had reached his home safely. But then it led to other complications and the UDA had a review meeting.

I wanted to take revenge because there were so many people who had been murdered in my community. There had been many attacks on our pubs and clubs. Our conditioning was that if they killed one of us, then we killed ten of them. That was the reality and that was the way we were programmed.

Dicky, the Catholic who I'd known in Hydebank, came out about two months after me. People told me that he was looking for me. So, I met up with him and we got a takeaway with a couple of girls. At midnight that night, two hooded men came round to the house and asked for Dicky. I told them that he was upstairs. They demanded that I brought him down as they'd been sent to shoot him. I told them that I was not going to get him and that they were not going to shoot him. I had a row with the men and put my life on the line in a sense. I knew who they were, but I stood up to them. I told them to clear off and that I would sort it out the next day. In the morning, I went to the UDA commander's house. "Listen, last night I brought a Roman Catholic in. This guy is not in the IRA, he is just an ordinary Catholic. He was inside Hydebank for a robbery," I said. They just warned me. "Don't let it happen again. You can't do that."

So, I know that I saved his life that night. I'm not saying that I was trying to redeem myself, but I knew in my own mind, that I had at least saved a life. I also knew from that moment on, I wouldn't be able to take someone's life again. I just wanted to know more about ordinary Catholics, because until I met Dicky, I never realised there was such a thing.

At that time, I started going out with a girl called Sally. We were in the Woodvale area, just having a chat at the edge of an entry, when the next minute, Anne Kennedy and another detective came up the entry. They were raiding the house where I was standing at the back door. Anne Kennedy, who knew who I was because of the UDA and past charges, asked if I wanted a lift home. I told her to go away. "Are you trying to get me shot for being an informer?" I said.

The following week I was out with my friends in Paisley Park, which is on the West Circular Road. In the back of my mind, because I'd had this friendship with a Catholic guy, I was not so committed to the organisation. I thought about what had happened to Dicky and me, and because of that I decided that I didn't want to be involved with the UDA anymore. I knew that I was in a vulnerable position because in my mind, I felt tormented. I knew that I was faced with a dilemma and I decided to head home. As I was walking along the West Circular Road, I thought of Ann Kennedy and the week before when she had been talking to me. When I reached the Ballygomartin Road, a thought came into my head that if I saw Anne Kennedy, I must stop the car. As I walked down the Ballygomartin Road, I saw a car coming, so I waved it down. Inside was Anne Kennedy and another detective. "Can you give me a lift down the Shankill Road?" I asked her. So, I got into the car.

We began the journey, when all of a sudden, I turned to her and said that it was me who had committed the murder of Alexander Reid.

Anne obviously knew about this murder and that I had never made a statement. My three friends had been charged with the murder and put in prison. "Do you realise what you are saying?" she replied. I said that I did. We drove to Tenant Street where I was arrested and then taken to Castlereagh Police Station, which is a famous interrogation centre. I made a statement that my three friends had been charged for the murder, but I was guilty. They were surprised because this was the first time that I had made a statement. They had been trying to get me for so long and here I was confessing. They must have wondered what was going on.

On June 16, 1981, I was charged with the murder of Alexander Reid at Castlereagh Station.

Chapter 6

Time On Your Hands

I was placed in remand in Crumlin Road Prison. It was built in the nineteenth century and designed by the renowned architect and engineer, Charles Lanyon. Built within a five-sided walled site, the gaol had four wings that fanned out from a central area known as The Circle, or Control Area. This was copied from Pentonville's *radial cellular system*, a blueprint reproduced in fifty-four other prisons. The gaol was built to house up to 550 prisoners in single cell accommodation, each cell measured 12 by 7 feet, and 10 feet in height. At the height of the Troubles three people shared a cell. By the time it closed in 1996, up to 25,000 prisoners had walked through its gates; including Jerry Adams, Rev. Ian Paisley and now me.

On my first night, they put me in a cell with a Roman Catholic. *Am I going to have to serve my time with a Roman Catholic?* I asked myself.

At this particular time, I still thought these people were the enemy. I decided not to fight because I had to share a cell with him. The next morning, I asked the guards why I had to share a prison cell with a Catholic. The prison guards had seemingly done it on purpose to see how I would react. Then they moved me into A-wing where there were both Protestants and Catholics. Initially, I shared a cell with men called Harpo and Big Chuck Berry. But then the prison officers moved Big Chuck Berry out of the cell and moved in a man called Frankie Curry.

During my time there, I ended up sharing cells with different people;

although they were all Loyalists. The practice was simply this — they put two or three of you in a cell, with three pots to go to the toilet in; it was very stuffy and cramped. You could not get the window open to let in fresh air and the windows were locked. During the summer, when it was really warm, I lay on my bed in my underwear; it was like a sauna. If there were three prisoners in a cell with weak bladders then you were in trouble. I have since heard that the prisoners who were in over-crowded cells have been given £2,500, as compensation because of the inhumane conditions.

The regime was difficult at this time. You had no time to yourself; there were always interactions with people. Because of the crowding and the threat of riots, prisoners were locked up for twenty-three hours each day. All I could do was talk to people if they wanted me to or I lay and dozed in a confused state. Initially, I was there for six months.

If we look at the history of the attacks on prison officers, most of it came from the Crumlin Road and The Maze prisons. This was because of the way the prison officers treated prisoners by locking them up for so long. Dogs were treated better.

If you were fortunate enough, your family sent you food such as cheese and meat, but you didn't receive it until the end of the night. It was left in a really warm place and the meat went off. Not only that, some of the prisoners from higher up urinated out of their windows and this landed on your meat. Unsurprisingly, that caused a lot of trouble as our parents struggled to earn money to bring us food parcels at various times.

Protestants and Catholics were allowed into the exercise yard on alternate days. I got out of my cell for one hour a day for exercise. I remember when I went into the yard, there was a small, grassed area by the wall; it was where the prisoners who had been executed in the years gone by were buried. It would have been part of their sentence to be buried in an unmarked grave, in unconsecrated ground.

The dining hall operated in exactly the same way. One day, it would be the Republicans who were allowed to eat in there, and the next day it was our turn. On the day you that were not allowed into the dining hall, you ate in your cell. It was de-facto segregation.

The prison officers only came on to the wing for an hour each day. They only came in to do a security check and a head count.

On a Monday morning, activities started at a quarter to seven with prison officers switching on lights and waking you up. Picture three guys in a cell; it is a quarter to eight in the morning. At half eight, quarter to nine, you were allowed out to throw a drop of water around your face, but you were not allowed a shower. You just got a wash, a drop of water around your face and armpits, to empty your pot, collect breakfast and then go back to your cell. Then you ate your breakfast and left your tray out. Well, it was difficult for me. Some people read books or did crosswords, but that was not for me, so I listened to the radio or shouted out of the windows, to get a general conversation going with other prisoners.

The object was to rile each other up in prison; it was a time bomb waiting to explode. Each night we sang Loyalist songs as loudly as we could as we thumped the door as if it was a big drum, to keep the Republicans awake. They retaliated by singing their Fenian songs and I think they out-sung us because we were out-numbered by them.

One night I remember singing, *One thousand green bottles hanging on the wall,* out of the window just to annoy the inmates. It nearly did my own head in.

Twenty-three hours was a very long time to be locked up and it was very difficult for me because I wasn't a reader or a writer. I often ended up on my own because I was always in trouble so I'd be taken to a punishment cell. I got through by sitting in my cell with my eyes closed, as I thought about where I lived on the Shankill. In my head, I went up the left-hand side of the road into all the pubs and into all sorts of different places; I remembered where everybody sat, their certain looks or should I say, certain ways.

After I had been up the left-hand side, I crossed over at the lights at the top of the road and went down the other side. That's how I kept my mind occupied until I learnt how to read later on, when I was twenty-five.

The Diamond Jubilee Bar was often visited by two ladies who sought to sell their services; some would call them *ladies of the night,* even though it was day time when they came.

Andy Knowles, who would have not been far from hitting the tender age of seventy, was another character in The Diamond. He sat and had a drink and minded his own business. The locals knew Andy had a trigger point and because of that, a local was ushered next to Andy's stool where he stood at the other side of their friend and waited for the opportune time. When Andy's head was turned the other way away, the guy shouted, and pretended it was coming from his friend who was sitting beside Andy. "Who shot the cobbler!" Then before the guy knew it, he was lying on his back on the bar floor. Andy had knocked him out with one punch.

Greenland Street hosted the illegal *pitch and toss*, created by my dad and my Uncle Robert, who was known as *Bubbly*. Between my father and Dougie McHood, they ran a series of illegal games in an entry, near Echo bookies. This enticed gamblers to partake in the *pitch and toss* when they went to and fro from the bookies. I was a child when they hired me to keep an eye out for the *drango*. Should the policeman on his motorbike appear my job was to shout, DRANGO, DRANGO! Everyone then scattered, and left the money on the ground before they went into Echo and closed the door.

In the Salisbury Bar, was an old character called Roy, who was known as the *human shredder*. He sat and ripped up paper or bookie documents or newspaper into the smallest pieces you could ever imagine. You always knew where Roy would be sitting because pieces of paper surrounded the stool. These reflections helped me to keep my sanity.

I have to say that it was never a dull place in the Crumlin Road — there were weapons smuggled in, attempted escapes, and the SAS came in and out at night — obviously up to something. Both of the opposing paramilitaries remained absolute in that we were not criminals, but we were in fact political prisoners. Among our own communities, we were known as POWs (Prisoners of War).

A couple of Loyalist prisoners in the Crumlin Road Prison once planned an escape. When they tried to get into the circle in the prison, they were spotted by a prison officer who hit the alarm. This meant that they had to take the prison officers hostage and put them into the dining hall.

However, they were never going to be successful with their escape, so one of them came and got me out of my cell. He stood with me on the two's landing on A-wing, with a gun to my head. There was a lot of tension and many implications as soldiers with rifles arrived on the wing. 'I've got them in sight, shall I open fire?' one soldier shouted into his radio as they stood on the one's landing. "Under no circumstances open fire because there are hostages in the dining hall," was the reply.

This was a traumatic experience for me. I didn't know what was going on at the time and I didn't know that the soldier wasn't going to open fire. If the shot was fired, it probably would have hit me because I was in the line of fire. Thankfully, the gun siege was resolved peacefully and nobody was killed. My friends who attempted the escape were eventually charged.

What we wanted was legal segregation as opposed to de-facto segregation.

I realise this means that we wanted the Republicans to go into one wing and the Loyalists into another. We did not want to associate with the enemy, nor did they wish to associate with us.

Crumlin Road Prison riots, Oso wearing checked jacket.

It came to a head when the commanders of the Loyalists in A and C wings decided that enough was enough and that they had no other option but to take hostages. They decided that we needed to show the prison officials who were the real bosses and take over the prison. We felt that we had no other choice because of the pressure that we were being put under, not to mention being outnumbered by the Republicans.

Because the Republicans were high in number, they dictated what was happening. It was like the majority and minority rule. On remand, there wasn't any work, so this added to the tension, and caused a lot of fights. Moreover, the prison authorities, were not very forthcoming in giving us extra association or television time, and this increased the tension even more.

The orders were given — take over the prison. I knew that when we did this, we would be entering the protection wing where there were sex offenders, gangsters and corrupt policemen. The prisoner who used to purposely urinate over our food was a sex offender and we decided that it was time to teach him a lesson; although when we went to his cell, he had been released.

We planned and organised among ourselves to go on to the roof and protest. I was eighteen and I was excited about it. I was also frightened because previously when a number of prisoners had tried to escape, guns had been smuggled in, and as I've mentioned, the SAS had also been seen on the wing with guns and hoods on.

First, we planned to take A and C wing together after the church service when everyone was making their way back onto the wing. We were going to take over both wings and then take the Protestant prisoners to the roof. This did not happen. The commander was supposed to shout the order for the rest of C-wing to leave the church and rush into A-wing. He did not give the order. It was all planned to happen on a Sunday, but it did not happen. There were thirteen people on my landing and we had a meeting on Sunday afternoon. We were annoyed that the order had not been given for the other wing to come. We felt we were psyched up for it; we were ready.

We needed to do something because the pressure was building up. So, all the Loyalist prisoners decided to take matters into our own hands and planned to take A-wing for ourselves. We waited until Thursday evening at 5:30 p.m., when we would be getting out for association. I remember coming out of my cell and seeing someone with a hood come out of the toilet. The hooded man pointed a gun at the prison officer. I ordered the prison officer to give me the keys, then I opened the cell, locked the prison officer in the cell and proceeded to let out all the Loyalist prisoners. We were on the twos which was the middle landing. There were also the ones and threes. My job was to get the keys to the grill that led from the twos to the ones. It was okay from the ones to the twos because there were wooden stairs. No one was going anywhere until I could open the grill. I was standing with a bunch of keys with thirty or forty people screaming at me to open it. This caused me to panic; I didn't know which key to use to open the grill.

Out of frustration I told everyone to get out of the way. I took a dive at the gate to bust it open. I remember bouncing back and falling on my back. As I was lying on the ground, I kicked the lock with all my force. The grill collapsed and we ran up the stairs.

The plan was to get twelve men on the roof and lock everyone else in their cells.

I had warned my family that I would be going up, and I told them to be outside with the camera, and that we would be coming out around tea-time. When we got everybody up on the landing there were two fellas on the wing. On one side of the three's landing, there were prisoners who were on protection. There were policemen such as a detective sergeant, who later got acquitted, sex offenders and various hoods. While I was doing that, the men got onto the roof. We'd taken the keys off the prison officers, so I opened the cells of all those who were on protection and asked them to throw their mattresses out to barricade the stairs and the landings. I got them to wreck their cells and dig holes in the wall. The entire prison was wrecked. They used bed ends to make holes into every cell wall so that you could walk from one end of the wing right down to the other through the cells. Then we turned on the big fire hydrant and flooded the wing.

With the wing wall secure, everyone mingled on the threes. I wanted to get on the roof. At first, our commanders would not let me up, but I insisted. We got onto the roof and started to dismantle it by throwing the roof tiles onto the prison guards below in the yard. Crowds started to gather on the street outside and I saw my mum. Proud as punch, I stood there waving and shouting at her.

For so long, we had taken so much with the government's policy of criminalisation. Within the Loyalist movement, we felt as if we were political prisoners; the hunger strike had already taken place. The government's policy was, in my view, to treat us badly.

The Protestants and Catholics were never allowed in the dining hall together and it was the same for exercise. The wings were mixed, though not usually the cells. Yet, you could have Protestants in one cell and Catholics in the adjacent cell. And that was why in 1981, we went on to the roof; we wanted segregation and improved facilities.

No-one had thought about checking the weather, and it just so happened that the night we were on the roof, it was the coldest night in fifty years in Belfast; it literally started snowing.

The prison guards who were being held by us, were kept confined in one cell so that they would understand our experiences as prisoners.

When they heard that we were holding hostages, the prison authorities went into negotiations quickly to see what they could do to get them released. Our first request was food for the wing and for the hostages.

They received a bar of chocolate and two cigarettes between them. One of the guard's wives was pregnant and because he did not know what the outcome would be, he asked for permission to write a letter to his wife. His request was granted, but just as they censored our letters, we also censored and edited his.

The second part of the operation was then put into action — to release a number of Republicans from their cells because they had been incarcerated for thirty hours. Several others, me included, opened their cells on the ones and twos, and put them into the dining hall. Fear showed in their faces; they were unsure what was going to happen to them.

The leadership had a meeting with the Republicans and they were frightened. They felt that we could go into their cells and kill them one by one. There were negotiations, but in the dining hall, they got their own morale up.

On the second day, the prison authorities switched off the electricity, but we were ready for that. We had prepared marble tins filled with butter to use as candles. Throughout the night we sang songs to keep up our spirits. Outside bonfires were being lit in support and a local Loyalist band paraded up and down the street. There was a real sense of unity being shown that we were all in this together. Our plight was in every newspaper.

On the third day, there were more negotiations. The authorities asked us if we would release some of the prison officers. They promised that they would move us to better conditions. We released a few of the prison officers and then after the third day, we released the rest of the prison officers when we decided to end the protest.

However, the authorities were adamant that they were not going to go into the prison until the weapons were removed. We assured them that we had none, but nevertheless, they would not come on to the wing for six hours.

They requested that we return to our cells and when we did, they handcuffed us. We were brought down to the ones which was littered with lockers, desks and mattresses. There was temporary lighting and it was cold. Prison guards stood watching us with their vicious dogs.

We were then brought out and given food, before being transferred to C-wing.

In the middle of the night, the horse boxes, special vans that had one person per cubicle, arrived. All the remand prisoners were put into the vans and taken to another famous prison, The Maze, otherwise known as H-Block. They had promised better conditions, but they did not keep their word.

At this time, I lived for the paramilitaries. We did what we did in the Crumlin Road to survive. We stood together regardless of which Loyalist organisation we belonged to.

Chapter 7

The Maze (H-Block)

On October 5, 1981, the local newspaper, reported that sixty-four people were murdered during the seven-month, hunger strike, terror campaign run by the IRA. During this period the hunger strike protest impacted within The Maze and the community.

They included:
- 12 RUC personal (Royal Ulster Constabulary)
- 3 RUC Reservists
- 8 Soldiers
- 7 UDR (Ulster Defence Regiment)
- 34 Civilians

Against such a background, tensions were very high within the prison and the broader community. The tension in the prison was also made up of the propaganda that the IRA was mustering in the wider community — that they were the victims and not the ones who they were inflicting death and destruction. In the midst of all of this, the Loyalist prisoners appeared to be forgotten about.

The key dates in the Crumlin Road Prison Protest of 1981:

1. Friday October 2, 1981, there was a gun siege in Crumlin Road Gaol. Armed prisoners staged a headline grabbing operation to highlight grievances about conditions in A-wing and demanded segregation and improved facilities.

2. Thursday December 10, 1981, the big protest action began with Loyalists in a sub-zero rooftop prison protest in the Crumlin Road.

3. Saturday December 12, 1981, the rooftop protest ended and prisoners were moved to The Maze in tin cans.

On June 20, 1981, my sister's birthday, I stood in Belfast Crown Court and charged with murder.

We were taken to H-Block 3, which is where the Republicans were held during their dirty protest, spreading their excreta on the walls using their hands. We were put into cells that weren't very clean and smelt.

Within a week the Protestants wrecked all those cells as well. We had been given guarantees that we were going to be put into better conditions and the issues that we were protesting about would be addressed. The prison authorities broke their promise. They promised us that they would deal with the issues and they went against everything that they said. They did not improve our conditions. Even though the cells were power-hosed down with water and chemicals, the stench still remained.

There were wire grills on the windows so you could not even open your window to get fresh air.

The Maze Prison was also called H-Block because of the wings that formed the buildings into the shape of an H. There were eight H-blocks in total and where the wings met in the middle of each block, there was a square, which was called *the circle*. The circle or square was an interesting feature; it was the meeting area. Any time that you were wanted by the principal officer or you had a visitor, you were called by your number. If I heard, "138 Calderwood to the circle," I went out and looked for a circle even though it was a square.

Because it was a high security prison and mainly held paramilitaries, the food was not allowed to be made on site because of the risk of cutlery being used for weapons. Instead, lorries arrived each day with the food. If you were with a visitor, your food was put on a hot plate to keep warm.

The whole scenario started again. They had put us on to the wing with Republicans and in worse conditions. The government had gone back on our demands. We wanted to rebel immediately because of the block that we were put in.

We got together and had a meeting. We decided that the only course of action we could take was to start the whole process over again and wreck the wing. Our demands had not been met — we had been hoodwinked, which seems to be a common thread with British establishment.

We sent word to the commander on the blocks, Jimmy Craig. We explained that because of the conditions we were going to wreck the wing. He panicked. "Don't be doing anything. Everything is okay," he said. The reality was that he was in the hospital wing, which was clean, but we were in the dirty wings of C and D. He hadn't seen the conditions we were living in.

Two Loyalist prisoners then decided to go on hunger strike because of the situation. Right from the start, our commander and leadership were against the hunger strike because they realised that there were ten Republican hunger strikers who were already dead. We felt that we were in the Republican shadow. It seemed as if the government always bowed to Republicanism, but did not listen to the Loyalist or Protestant voice in the prison. This made us angry and our hunger strike went on. The guys who went on the hunger strike were 100% genuine. They would have been prepared to go through with it, but it was the leadership that would not let us do it. The results of the IRA hunger strike showed that it was never going to work. The commander told the hunger strikers to end it. The UDA and the UVF were united at this time, because they wanted segregation.

In the face of adversity, we had a common enemy, the British Government. They were trying to deny us our rights. It seemed crazy to me, that the very thing we were fighting for, was to protect our British identity, yet the British Government were turning on us. We were being punished for protecting our own community of police and soldiers. It is ironic that the very people who we were protecting were the ones who had arrested and imprisoned us. They were the people we had fought for. We felt they had let us down. They were going to impose all these things on us. We called ourselves Loyalists to the queen and the Crown, and we were being punished for it. It was policemen, soldiers and ordinary civilians; the people from our community who were being murdered. Our people were being terrorised and killed, and we wanted to counter this by taking revenge.

Six months passed and it was nearly time for me to head back to C-wing, at Crumlin Road. I had been on remand all this time and now I had to be transferred back to await my trial. That was the way they operated in those days. Anyone who was on remand went to The Maze and once you got to the stage that you were awaiting trial, you were transferred to C-wing at the Crumlin Road Gaol.

It was possible to walk away free from remand, if there was not enough evidence against you. If you got charged with murder, it could take eighteen to twenty-four months to await trial. So, you'd be stuck in prison for fourteen months and even if you were innocent, then that was unfortunate, but at least you would have completed fourteen months of your sentence.

My six months in The Maze before I returned to the Crumlin Road was centred on the campaign of de-facto segregation. We imposed our own segregation and the authorities were happy to go along with this. We were in a mixed wing with the Republicans and we were outnumbered. It was D-wing of H-Block 3. The remand blocks were H-Block 3 and H-Block 6.

1) H-Block, Longkesh, Maze, all names of the infamous prison that housed paramilitaries.

Even though we were on the same wing, we imposed self-segregation. In the morning, the Republicans went out and had a wash, then went to exercise. Then the Loyalists went for a wash, while the Republicans were out to exercise in the yard. On one day, the Republicans ate their dinner in the dining room, and we ate our dinner in our cells. Then at tea-time, we had our tea in the dining room and they ate their tea in their cells. We never ate together, mixed together or associated together.

At night time, it was either Republicans or Loyalists in the television room. One or the other.

The rooftop protest in the Crumlin Road of 1981, had not achieved anything. There were promises made, especially when spokesmen from organisations became involved with the government and negotiated on what they felt the five demands were that had to be met. But nothing was met and this continued. I don't think that any of the demands were met. For a start, the politicians were not allowed to come in. They might have taken some to the visiting area, but only one person was allowed to visit. We needed the politicians to come on to the wing to see the conditions that we were living in. We wanted them to see the regime we were under, but this was not allowed at that particular time.

We wanted the visits to be changed.

The government's policy of criminalisation took effect. When you went through the prison doors it all depended on what you were charged with, as to which part of the prison you were put in. If someone was coming in for a bank robbery, for example, they would log them on as an ordinary decent criminal (ODC) and put them into protection.

We were not trying to imply that we did not need protection. What we had done, we had done to raise money for weapons. The prison system was a political system. The hunger strikes happened because they wanted political status. The government took away that political status although they accepted that there were political prisoners and people who were treated differently. I think that is the reason why we had the Diplock courts[15]. If you were charged with a terrorist offence, you did not have a jury trial. That proved that people were different.

They were saying that there were no such things as political prisoners.

The reality was; however, that there were political prisoners. There were people who went on hunger strikes, yet people were saying that nothing had changed. These issues have been happening from 1969, and they continue today. Then all of a sudden, the government changed their policy and tried a new initiative called criminalisation. So, obviously both Republicans and Loyalists were going to rebel against that.

---

15 Diplock courts were criminal courts in Northern Ireland for non-jury trials of specified serious crimes. They were introduced by the Northern Ireland Act 1973, and used for political and terrorism-related cases during the Troubles.

I returned to the Crumlin Road Prison in 1982, and it was back to the old routine. Because of what happened on the roof, I was treated differently. I felt that I was picked on by the prison officers. Again, I went back to C-wing and was put in charge of the wing, but I was not the commander of it. Our commander, Jimmy Craig, was still at The Maze. There could have been a method in their madness, but I was not good at articulating what I had to say; so, when I went to the governor with demands, it was demands I went with. Basically, if our demands weren't met, then destruction would follow.

I believe I was used as a puppet because I had the backbone to do something about our issues. Even though there were a few who were good at talking, they did not want to put themselves to the fore. They just wanted to use brute force, so they sent me instead. This led to me being locked up in a cell. I was put on my own in a cell and I had loss of privileges for thirty days. This meant that they took my radio and I wasn't allowed to go to the tuck shop, have parcels or visitors.

Lock-up was 8 o'clock at night. When the prison guards had gone, I signalled to the prisoners above me, so they could put a radio in a pillowcase and lower it down to me. I listened to the radio and send it back up first thing in the morning so that I didn't get caught with it. They also sent me food and chocolate; we looked out for each other.

Chapter 8

The Maze, a Training Camp

My trial was held in April, 1982, at the High Court in Belfast. I decided that I was going to fight this case the whole way. I believed that it was a challenge and I wanted to fight the system. I was steeped in paramilitarism, but there were dilemmas in my life about whether all Catholics were Republicans. That is one of the dilemmas about Richard McCann. Not all Catholics were in the PIRA. Because I was with the Loyalists, those who wanted to fight and protect their country, I had to fit into the role again. I did not become who I was meant to be, the Oso of today; instead, I became someone else to keep everyone happy.

I was brought into the dock and sat down with prison officers surrounding me. I had to sit through the trial and listen to people telling lies about me. The Crown prosecutor kept pointing out that I was a member of the UDA among other things. I remember becoming irate.

"Look, you little ****. Who is on trial here?" I said.

"Don't be using language like that in my court," said the judge.

I explained that I wanted to make a point. "Who is on trial here? Is it the UDA or is it me because this wee clown here, keeps on referring to the UDA," I said to the court.

I never denied being a member of the UDA, but it was me who was on trial. The judge then turned to the Crown prosecutor and told him to refer to me as Mr Calderwood and not to mention the UDA. I had made my point.

To be fair, I knew that I had told a few lies in my statement. I had made statements admitting other things during my time in Castlereagh. But strangely enough, the statements went missing; they never appeared with the transcripts. Simply because, the things I admitted happened while I was in the Young Offenders Centre. They caught on to this at the last minute. The police had used so-called interviews I had given in the Young Offenders Centre against me and used them as corroborative evidence. The fact was that I had never given any interviews in Hydebank Young Offenders Centre. So, I said to my solicitor, "What we need to do here is to bring in the two prison officers who took me to the interview. They will be able to prove conclusively that I did not give this interview and it will prove that, that man there is telling lies." My solicitor said that I did not need to do it. But I felt that it was crucial.

He should have done it; he did not do it and I lost my case. That was one of the reasons.

The second reason was that another policeman, who had stopped me at the scene of the crime, spoke up. He had made a note of the clothes that I was wearing and obviously the clothes that I was wearing at the time of the crime; just as it happened, within the space of twenty minutes, after the police had found the body. The clothes mentioned in the statement were not the clothes that this policeman said I was wearing when he stopped me at the scene of the crime. It was very strange that the page from his notebook had gone missing. I know that I am uneducated, but even so. When the judge found me guilty and sentenced me to life in prison, I laughed at him.

"Mr. Calderwood, what do you find funny?" he asked.

"Your Honour, it shows me how much you are not interested in the trial, when you have just sentenced me to life and it is something that you cannot do. That is the reason I am laughing. I told you that I was under eighteen years of age at the time of the crime and therefore, you cannot give me life," I replied.

The Judge became very irate and said that he would defer the sentence.

He would sentence me to the Secretary of State's pleasure. This was a junior life sentence and because I was under the age of eighteen, I could not be sentenced to a set number of years.

However, what I could not believe, was that the judge didn't seem interested in me at all because he did not even look at my age, at the time he was passing sentence.

If I hadn't have said anything; however, I could have had a re-trial. There were so many people going through the system at the time, that you were not treated as a human being, but merely a number. Did anyone care how I had been brought up? Did anyone realise how I became involved in the conflict? Did anyone consider why I had turned out the way I had?

I was faced with an unfair system. And, of course, this was a Diplock court. Therefore, I was not entitled to a jury trial. Hadn't British justice been given to terrorists around the world? I felt angry and resentful that it was one law for one and one law for another.

For the first time in my life, I felt that I might never leave prison again.

I knew that I had been sentenced to the Secretary of State's pleasure and I did not know how many years you endured before getting out.

'I could die in prison,' I said to myself for the first time in my life. It was real. I had just been sentenced and I thought that because I was going from one regime to another, they did not know what to do with me because I had been sentenced at the Secretary of State's pleasure.

My father and mother were still coming to terms with the fact that I had murdered someone, in fact, they were in shock that this was happening. As they sat with family, watching their son being charged with murder, I knew I had also taken principles from their life; my family burst into tears as my sentence was read out.

2) H-Block, Longkesh, Maze, all names of the infamous prison that housed paramilitaries.

The Secretary of State had to sign a document so that I could be transferred to The Maze Prison. This would take about thirty days, so they took me to the punishment cells. I was locked up again for twenty-three hours a day, with just one hour's exercise. I remember a friend who was sentenced to eighteen months in prison. He happened to be on one of the landings above the punishment cells. I remember lying at night and shouting up to him, "Am I going to have to stay like this for the rest of my sentence?"

I did not know what it was to be a sentenced prisoner. It was frightening to think about it when I was lying in my cell. The fella I shouted up to reassure me. He said that I would be okay once I was in The Maze. "You will get to be with the rest of the prisoners, hang on in there," he said. He was very encouraging.

After the first week, I got a visit from my mother and one of the counsellors from the local area. I spoke to them about the situation that I'd found myself in and my mother started crying. Obviously, it was upsetting for both of us and the counsellor tried to reassure me and my mother that things would get better. He said that he would try to arrange a meeting with the prison governor to see what he could do for me.

This lasted for another two weeks while they investigated why I was in this situation because I had not been convicted of any crime within the prison system. They then agreed to put me on to D-wing with the sentenced prisoners. They would put me on to the regime until it was time to be transferred to The Maze Prison. I was nineteen.

I knew many of the prisoners and the majority were doing life sentences.

There were men there who I looked up to in my community, who were my heroes. Finally, I was going on to D-wing where there was a routine.

I began to understand the prison system. I did not look on myself as an ordinary decent criminal. I looked on myself as a political prisoner, although I did not understand all the ins and out of being political. I did what I did for the protection of my community.

Finally, it happened. The Secretary of State signed the forms that enabled me to be sent to The Maze Prison. I had been at the Crumlin Road Gaol for a year and a half on and off because of my involvement in the rooftop protest on A-wing. I had been sent to The Maze as a remand prisoner and then back to the Crumlin Road to await my trial, before being sent to The Maze as a sentenced prisoner.

When I arrived at The Maze this time, I was put with the YPs (young prisoners). I was considered a YP, because I was still in my teens. The governor at the time said that I had to stay with the YPs until I was twenty-three and then I could be moved in with the men. So, I asked for a meeting with him.

"Listen, I want to be moved in with the men now," I said.

"Calderwood, you're in jail. You'll be told what to do," he replied.

I was undeterred. "No, I won't be doing what I'm told. I want to be moved in with the men and if you don't move me into your wing then I am going to bust all your windows, all your toilets and your sinks. I'm going to wreck your whole wing if you don't move me in with the men."

So, the Governor thought about it. "Well, there's only one way that I can move you in with the men at the age you are, and that is to put you down as unruly," he said eventually.

I was satisfied with that. "Well, that'll do."

So, they put me down as unruly and I got moved to C-wing on H-Block 3. There were about forty-seven men; thirty-eight Republicans and nine Loyalists. We were outnumbered by about four to one.

On C-wing, the cells were numbered from 3 to 26. They were all single cells, measuring 9 feet by 6 feet. Everyone was in a single cell and most of them had a double bed, apart from cell 26, which had two bunk beds. At long last, there was room. As well as your bed, there was a pot and a gallon of water, but there were bars over the window. The cell had a black floor with cream walls. The lighting was fluorescent, which I think damaged your eyes more than it helped. Later, when I learnt how to read and write, I asked them to turn off the light. I read with the light from the outside coming in. It was easier on my eyes. When you looked out of the window, all you could see was wire, corrugated iron and the lights of the exercise yard.

UDA on patrol in 90's

These were obviously very difficult times at The Maze Prison as I had just come from the Crumlin Road Gaol and we had been fighting for segregation. It wasn't any different at The Maze Prison and I continued to be unruly and disruptive. I was always challenging authority and doing the opposite to orders. As a consequence, the prison guards put me on a drug called Largactil. They said that I was always hyperactive and this drug was meant to calm me down. But the reality was that this was a tranquiliser for horses — I was receiving it twice a day. This went on for two and a half years without me being given any updated diagnosis. It wasn't long before I lay in bed late at night as I tried to go to sleep, but I couldn't because I had *electric shocks* in my head. A lot of the other prisoners were given sleeping tablets to calm them. Looking back, I am certain that I had what is now commonly known as ADHD (attention deficit hyperactivity disorder). However, the drug didn't calm me down and I was still running around playing football. When I eventually managed to come off the drug, I started to have strange experiences which must have been the after effects. Throughout this time, no one ever asked how I was. Our general wellbeing and welfare as prisoners was never of any concern to the prison guards and that included our food supply.

The Republican prisoners stopped us eating in the dining hall due to the numbers they had, they overwhelmed us. We had to go into the dining hall, lift a couple of rounds of bread and a bit of meat and then go back to our cells. After six weeks of not having a warm meal, we were fed up. All the Republicans had gone over to another wing in exchange for others. It was a Saturday afternoon; sausage rolls and beans were on the menu for tea. We got into the kitchen first and saw all the sausage rolls and beans that were left on the hot plate. I was absolutely starving. "Get these into you," I said to the lads. We were famished and ate the lot, but as a result there were none left for the Republicans. Inevitably, that caused a riot.

We had to be prepared at all times. The Republicans were planting bombs behind radiators in the dining halls in Crumlin Road Prison, while in The Maze they planted fire bombs in Loyalist cells. It was a very frightening experience and put everyone on edge. When they put a fire bomb underneath a prisoner's bed, it exploded. A couple of people nearly died just from the smoke inhalation.

The Republicans made the bombs inside their cells. They used large tins from the kitchen that had contained jam, and put petrol in them before they made a sentry device designed to explode in the cell. Invariably, it caught the mattress on fire. There were a couple of people who were very fortunate not to have been killed as a bomb went off in their cell.

Thankfully, they were alright because the officers caught them in time.

After being on protest for eighteen-and-half months the boys were sitting having a conversation about why we were on protest for segregation.

Then one guy spoke up and said, "Sure we have segregation!"
That coming Monday morning all the Loyalists put their name down to see the Governor of the prison to inform him that the protest was over.

This in turn caused a dilemma for the prison authorities. As a response, the Governor decided to take ten Loyalists and ten Republicans and put them into the same Wing.

As soon as the authorities opened the cell doors the opposing fractions beat the life out of each other. That stopped any further segregation.

Contrary to popular belief that Republicans achieved segregation through their dirty protest and hunger strike. No, it was the Loyalists who achieved it as the Republican protests had ended a lot earlier.

During this time in The Maze, I felt as if I was living in a bubble. I became institutionalised with a mundane routine; it was the same procedure every day. My life stood still. People say prison is a good preserver; they're right. You don't have the worries of paying rent or electric, phone and bills. There is no concern about where your next meal is coming from or when you need to buy clothes. These are worries avoided by every prisoner.

What did happen; however, was that these worries were transferred to my parents. They were the ones who had to scrimp and save, even beg from their friends, to get me what I needed. My parents were very good to me, but in all honestly, I don't think that I appreciated it enough at the time.

In my bubble, as a Protestant, a Loyalist, a political prisoner, a number (not Alex or Oso), I felt that I had to be someone who was not afraid to use violence towards others, including the prison guards. I couldn't allow myself to be dictated to by other prisoners. I had to be someone who was prepared for anything, regardless of the consequences.

When I was alone in my cell, I looked straight into the sky. I had always wanted to see a shooting star. It was one of the things that I always used to look for. "Well God, if you are there, show me a shooting star," I said one night. If I could have seen one, I felt it would have given me hope. I needed something to hold on to. I did see one that night and the next night. I began to believe that there was a God out there because I saw those shooting stars.

I had no idea how long I would be in prison, but I would serve my sentence until I could get out. There were several prisoners who were not content to serve their sentence and wanted to escape. The escape of the Republicans happened on September 25, 1983. They had been planning it during the summer. Somehow, they managed to smuggle handguns and knives into the prison. Then on a Sunday, the quietest day of the week, they took over the circle of H-Block 7 while they were carrying out their cleaning duties. The circle contained the operations room and once they took that over, they had control of the whole block.

After securing unarmed prison officers in nearby rooms, they hijacked the kitchen lorry. Thirty-seven prisoners hid in the back of the truck, while their ringleader hid in the passenger footwell and directed the driver at gunpoint towards the front gates as if they were returning from the kitchens.

Unfortunately, the next set of prison officers were arriving for their shift. They intercepted the lorry by blocking the entrance with their cars. The Republicans were determined and bolted out of the back of the truck in a last-ditch attempt to escape to freedom. While some managed to climb the fence and escape on foot, many of the prison guards were badly injured and sadly one died.

When The Maze escape happened there was fear — fear of what would happen if the Republicans took control. They were prepared to go to any lengths to escape. Even though they had escaped, almost half of them were recaptured within twenty-four hours. It took a little longer for the rest to be found as a few managed to flee to other countries including their safe haven — the Republic of Ireland.

I have come to realise that prison officers have a job to do, but a number of the prisoners made it very difficult for them. It is sad to think that lives was lost and injuries were suffered because men were doing their jobs.

In the eighties, prisons were not the same as they are today. Back then, the prison was a training camp for terrorism and what you didn't know before you were able to learn inside. The whole object of the time served then was that you would come out a better leader, more ruthless and more deadly — a better terrorist. The prison of today is to renew your mind, give hope, improve a person, all of which I favour one hundred per cent.

Chapter 9

No More Orders

In 1985, my life turned a corner. When you're in prison, you have a lot of time to reflect. I still hadn't learnt how to read and write properly, and I realised that I might be able to do something about that while I was inside. I had heard that there was a guy called Jackie McArthur from Bangor, Northern Ireland, who visited the prison on a regular basis. He was a pastor and ran a project called Outreach to Prisoners.

It was an initiative designed to build friendships and share the gospel with prisoners. Jackie was a great guy, he visited me and a lot of the other prisoners and spent time with us. It was called an ecclesiastical visit, which was an extra visit so you were still able to have your regular weekly visits from your family. I struck up a good friendship with Jackie and he was a great help. On his visits, he talked about this man called Jesus in a way that I had not heard before. Jackie gave me a Bible and I did a short Bible course with him. He told me about the Emmaus Bible courses, which interested me, so, in 1986, I started to do those too. Emmaus was a correspondence course that I could complete with Jackie's help. He read the Bible with me and talked about its relevance.

When Jackie shared Jesus with me, I did not feel condemned, even though I realised that I was a sinner. I learnt that Jesus had been sent from His Father to save the lost, including sinners like me. He loved others and had a message of hope.

My ability to read and write was improving all the time, but I needed extra help in this area, so I approached the governor and asked if I could have a remedial teacher. I thought that if I had someone to teach me, then I could learn how to read and write properly. He agreed and I was given two teachers called Gillian and Valerie. Gillian began the long process of teaching me how to read and write. Valerie was an art teacher and taught me how to draw. Finally, I had started to get an education.

It was June 3, 1987. I was in my cell and had just finished one of the Bible studies. I put the light out to go to sleep and was lying on my bed. I had a lot of questions and I tried to answer them. I thought, after all that I had done, where did I stand before God? As this process was going on in my mind, I began to think about my past life.

I looked back to when I was sixteen, when I went over to Scotland in a boat and contemplated committing suicide. I had both feet over the rail ready to jump in. But something stopped me. Was it God?

I looked back to what happened on the Ballygomartin Road, when the thought came into my head about speaking to Anne Kennedy. Again, I believed that this was God's hand upon my life.

It did not happen by coincidence. I believed in a thing called the sovereignty of God.

In Glencairn, a guy pulled out a gun one night and fired a couple of rounds at me. He pointed the gun in my face. I hit his hand and the gun went off and the bullet went through my hair. I had hair in those days. I know I should have died that night, but I believe God had his hand on my life.

Another time, I had a car accident. I had been driving at eighty miles per hour. It took four hours to get my friend out of the car. I know that I should have died that night as well, but God had his hand on my life.

Bothers in Arms

In prison I had been absorbing Bible studies and reading about this person called Jesus Christ. I read how he had left Heaven, and came down to Earth and died on a cross for sinners. I learnt that Jesus did that to save me, that He died for me willingly and that He saved me by His grace.

Here I was, lying on my bed in a cell; a sinner going to hell. I knew I deserved it. So, I got on my knees by my bed and asked the Lord Jesus Christ to come into my life. I became a Christian that night at 11 p.m. This was a new beginning and I felt happy about it. For the first time in my life, I could make decisions for me. Before this, my whole life had been lived to please the paramilitaries and other people. I was twenty-five; I knew I had been saved and that was the watershed in my life.

I also knew that I had to start taking orders from a new commander.

That commander was the Lord Jesus Christ. I decided that I was going to do what *He* wanted me to do, not what the paramilitaries wanted me to do. That was the challenge for me.

Later on in my life, I wrote a tract[16] with the intention of sharing my testimony and the gospel of the good news of Jesus, with others. Here is an extract of what I wrote:

> "I was without Christ and without hope. I got out of my bed and knelt down in my cell, there in the darkness I received the wonderful gift of salvation through Jesus Christ, I knew that the blood of Jesus Christ, God's son cleanseth us from all sin. (1 John 1:7) There were no flashing lights or heavenly visions but the Bible bears record that the angels in Heaven rejoiced that night. The Great Shepherd of the sheep had found another wandering lamb and carried him home that night. I lay back on my bed and laughed, it was the holy laughter of Abraham when he received God's promise. I too, had received a promise, *Whosoever shall call upon the name of the Lord shall be saved* Romans 10:13. Then I wept, it was with a mixture of emotions, after twenty-five years I had been released from the slavery of sin. They were tears of joy, but after a life lived in rebellion to God they were tears of repentance and sorrow. For so long I'd wandered far from God, but now I was home. In closing this testimony, all I would like to say is, if you as yet don't know the Lord Jesus Christ as your personal Saviour, then I urge you to seek Him today.
> Jesus says in John 14:6: *I am the way, the truth, and the life, no man cometh unto the Father, but by me.*
> *So come to Jesus today, as tomorrow is promised to no one.*

---

16 A Christian tract is a small leaflet that contains the Word of God, a gospel message and a call to faith at the end. They are often produced in large quantities and are designed to be shared easily with others.

The very next day, after I got down on my knees the previous night and asked Christ into my life, I remembered that I was still on a paramilitary wing. Each organisation had their own commander and I answered to the UDA. I went to the OC, the officer commanding, who was the UDA paramilitary leader of my wing.

"From today, I won't be taking any more orders. I am a Christian now. If you want to boot me out of the wing you can, but I will not be taking any more orders," I said.
He replied that he would not boot me out of his wing, but that he would take things as they came. I knew what they were saying behind my back. "Give him a week and he will be back to his old self again."

Thank the Lord, that was a long time ago and the grace of God, which saved me then has kept me to this day. The sovereignty of God was in control of my life and in control of what I was doing; He was my very breath. In the scriptures, it says, *My times are in your hand; deliver me from the hand of my enemies, and from those who persecute me.* Psalm 31:15, NKJV. The *times* refers to our circumstances in life, regardless of how we view them.

My times were in His hands. My very next breath was controlled by God because we can do nothing without him. He is sovereign and in control. God is the Maker who created the universe and he created all the creatures in the universe and mankind. One day we will need to answer to our Creator. We are not just born and left to our own devices. There is a God upon a throne; a God who rules this universe; no matter what men may think.

That was a big turning point in my life and it led to a lot of other challenges. Because Christ loved me, then I knew that I had to love others. I had been protesting for eighteen and a half months on the wing to get separated from people and I felt that God was saying to me, "Now listen, you can't be half-hearted here, you're going to have to be wholehearted."

I knew that my first week of being a committed Christian wasn't going to be easy. I was expected to behave differently. Christianity was about repentance; turning around. If you are walking one way down a road, blinkered, then you will just go straight forward in a blinkered way. You will be limited and confined to your path. But when you have a personal relationship with God, Christ says that you have to respect other people. You have to be different. If you don't know what repentance is; for me it was simple.

Looking back and being ashamed. Looking within and desiring change. Looking forward and accepting Christ into my daily walk.

Now that I was a Christian, I was faced with a lot of dilemmas because there was always someone who attempted to wind me up; they did it on purpose. However, this did not faze me and by the end of the week, I was heading towards maturity. I did not respond in the way that I usually responded — with violence. If someone said something untoward, I ignored it. "Well, Jesus loves you too," I replied. That was not easy, but it was a learning process. It was something that did not come overnight. I still made mistakes. I was human. Yes, there were times when I got angry, when people were trying to wind me up. What I realised that I had to do was pray and then God helped me. The scriptures teach us, that when we are weak, then we can be strong in him.[17]

So, the difficulty was that I was going to have to leave the Loyalist wings and go to what were called the mixed wings where there were Loyalists/Protestants and Republicans/Catholics in cells next to each other. I couldn't pick and choose who I was going to love. I had to go to the governor and say that I wanted to go on to the mixed wings.

Because of the life that I'd had on the Crumlin Road and the rooftop protest, the segregation campaign and all the wrecking and ruin that I had done, the authorities were a little bit sceptical. "What is this

---

17 2 Corinthians 12:10.

big lad at here? He's just been protesting to get separated and now he wants to go on the mixed wing," they said because they were convinced that I was up to something. They thought that I was going to cause havoc on the mixed wings. They didn't want to move me down at first because of their rules.

A lot of the inmates were testing and tempting me; it caused me a lot of hassles. I was eventually moved to the mixed wings in 1988. I began to mix with the Catholics, the Protestants and the ordinary decent criminals. As previously mentioned, we considered ourselves political prisoners, but the ODCs were prisoners who were inside for a common offence.

It was about this time that I put in for a transfer to Maghaberry Prison. This was a new prison in Lisburn that had opened in 1986. The HMP Maghaberry was built on an old RAF airfield which had originally been used as a flying station. It initially held all female prisoners, those on remand, and young offenders following the closure of the women's prison at Armagh. The male prison opened its gates to prisoners late in 1987, and it became fully integrated and was considered a high security prison. It is one of the few that is still in operation today.

It was while I was in Maghaberry, that I received a letter from my old Sunday School teacher, Mrs Snowdon. She had heard that I had become a Christian and she sent me a cutting from her diary. It read that I had been expelled from Sunday School and it showed a date in 1969. "Been praying for you ever since," her note said. It was wonderful to think that this lady had recorded it in her diary and had prayed for me all those years.

After the encouragement of that letter, I sent a request to Tim Chapman to visit me because I knew that I wanted to work with young people. I had known Tim all my life as he had been my probation officer when I was fourteen. When he visited me, I decided to challenge him. "Let me ask you this. When I was fourteen, you used to take young kids to see a football match but you never took me. "Why didn't you take me to one of those football matches?" I asked. "I was scared of you. You were a big lad and you were a bad lad," he replied. "Well, do you know that it really hurt me that you took all my friends to see football matches but you never took me," I said. That had an effect on him. He felt guilty that he had never taken me away and given me that opportunity.

There was a nun called Sister Genevieve, who often visited the prison.

She was the headteacher of St Louise's, a Catholic school on the Falls Road, Belfast. In 1992, when I was in Maghaberry, she came to visit a friend of mine. She saw me and came over to speak to me while I was eating my dinner. 'Are you a born-again Christian?' she asked. 'I am,' I replied. 'I can see it in your face,' she added. That was strange at the time, but she became a good friend. Later on, when the time came for me to be let out of prison, she sent for me. She invited me for dinner to her home on Malone Road. She said that she wanted to help me because she knew that I was under a lot of pressure after coming out of prison. She booked me a week's holiday in London and paid for everything, including the flights. She knew a lot of business people in Northern Ireland who all donated money to her for helping ex-prisoners in Northern Ireland. For example, when one ex-lifer came out of prison, she found him a flat in London. This man ended up being sponsored to go to university and completed a doctorate. Sister Genevieve made sure that his accommodation and flights were paid for so he could come back and visit his family. She did a lot of good work. It is unreal how I stopped hating Catholics and the very thing I hated, the Catholic Church. Sister Genevieve reached out to help me and I accepted her help. Her story can be found in several books.[18]

At Maghaberry, I was given the opportunity to continue my education. I took computer classes and similar courses. Then in 1993, I was released from Maghaberry Prison on a work scheme. Initially, you are allowed to come out for the weekend to gradually integrate you back

---
18 Sister Genevieve, published by Little, Brown Book Group, 2002.

into society. After a period of time, providing this goes well, you are released on full-time probation.

It was a Saturday and I had been released for the weekend. I was sitting with two lads having a coffee. "I'm going to have to go now because I'm going to be late for football," I said. I got up and walked past the building, literally sixty seconds before a bomb went off. It was the Shankill Road Bombing that happened on October 23, 1993. It turned out to be one of the most renowned incidents during the Troubles. The PIRA had targeted their attack on the leadership of the UDA, because they believed they were holding meetings above Frizzell's fish shop on the Shankill Road. They said that they had intended to clear the fish shop of civilians, but others said that they wanted their bomber to die because of his dealings with them. As the bomb was set down it went off and killed one of the bombers and nine bystanders. Fifty-seven others were badly injured. I've never talked about it before, but it destroyed me in a sense, because I was trying to put my life back together at the time. I would have been about thirty-two then.

Chapter 10

A New Lease of Life

When I was released on probation in 1993, I had an opportunity to complete the *Higher Force Challenge*. It was aimed at young people under the age of twenty-five but there were a few exceptions. It was a twelve-week course that ran on the Shankill Road in the old stadium centre and it was all about personal development and challenging young people in the area. It was also cross-community, so a group of about ten Protestants and ten Catholics were put in the same group.

The course included discussion groups, presentations, workshops and outdoor pursuits in the Pennines in England. There was an opportunity to take part in activities that included high ropes, parachute jumping and abseiling among many other activities. There were all kinds of interests that young people enjoyed. On completion of the course, I was presented with a certificate and I still have it in my house. It was a very rewarding experience and I got to meet several great people.

They're still running the course today and it's been going for forty years now. It has been very successful on both sides of the community and it enables many young people to obtain good careers and steers them in the right direction, and keeps them away from anti-social behaviour.

After that, I participated in the Stadium Youth Project, which was set up on the Shankill Road. This involves charitable work within the community. I wanted to help because I didn't want any young person to go through what I had been through. I wanted to do anything I could to stop that from happening. So, I came up with an idea.

There was a place called *The Centre,* on Conway Street on the Shankill. It was in a building that belonged to the Presbyterian Church. I approached the minister of the Westkirk Presbyterian Church in 1994, and I asked him if they would let me use their building as a drop-in centre. The building had not been in use for some time and was in desperate need of care and attention. I felt inspired to create a space for the unemployed during the daytime. I thought that it would be great if there was a place where people could come and get a cup of tea or coffee and have a chat. I also thought that it would be useful if I could help people sort out their benefits, fill out forms and apply for jobs or voluntary work. Between 1994 and 1996, I managed to fundraise £37,000 to refurbish the building.

When it was up and running, the drop-in was open to the public not only during the day but on a couple of nights as well. Then in 1996, I started up a mother and toddler's group. *The Daily Mirror* featured an article about it which attracted a lot of new mums to the area. They featured a picture of me on the front page holding a child, with the headline, *Safe in the Hands of a Killer.*

One day, the detective Anne Kennedy, came to visit me at *The Centre.*

She invited me to her home for dinner where I met her family. She then asked me if I would share my testimony to the young people who attended her church. I agreed and went to the Presbyterian Church.

Two guys called Walter and Derek were helping me at the time; they had been in prison. I used to visit them in prison and bring them food.

As soon as they were released, they came to help me in the drop-in centre. By that time, I had been running the centre for nearly eighteen months. The Presbyterian Church then approached me and offered to pay me for the work I was doing. They wanted to pay me £10,000 per year. But I told them that I didn't want it. I said that I was quite happy doing this voluntarily. However, I did inform them that I had two men assisting me. So, I suggested that they give the wage to Walter and Derek and split it between them.

Today, in 2022, Walter is still the manager of the centre. It opened all those years ago and it has been running for twenty-eight years.

In 1996, while I was still working in *The Centre*, I was approached by the Probation Board for Northern Ireland (PBNI). They asked me if I would like to work for them. This feels ironic now, as I ended up on probation for most of my life. They wanted to pay me a full-time wage of about £18,000 per year. I accepted their offer and they employed me for three years as a project worker to work with young people. I continued to work for them up until the year 2000. Tim Chapman turned out to be my boss as he was the assistant chief probation officer.

I was pleased that they had asked me to work for them, but I didn't really have any qualifications. I had completed computer courses, but I hadn't received any formal education such as O Levels or A Levels.

They agreed that I would need to go on a course, so they paid for me to go to university. I went to Jordanstown University and completed a Youth and Community Diploma. I passed with a commendation, or merit, and went on to do a theology degree which was a three-year course. So, that did my heart good, in a sense. I didn't expect to do as well as I did because of my lack of a formal education.

When I look back, the Probation Board did something that was unheard of — they employed six ex-Loyalist prisoners and six ex-Republican prisoners. They ran this project for three years, and employed ex-prisoners from both communities. It was a success in that out of the twelve people that they employed, ten ended up continuing their careers by working with young people.

There was a big school at the bottom of the Shankill Estate where I lived, called the Riddle. It was an old school and had been a youth club as well, but it was lying empty. So, as I had left *The Centre* and I was working for Probation, I approached the Belfast Education and Library Board (BELB). "Can I open that centre as a youth club for the area?" I asked them. Happily, they agreed and let me manage the club.

I was allowed to recruit about six part-time staff. I got that up and running at the same time that I was working for Probation. I worked for Probation during the day and for the youth club at night, with up to one hundred youths and with six volunteers. This happened in 1996, and continued for four years until the year 2000.

In 1996, I was asked to attend a youth conference in Liverpool Central Hall, in England, and share my testimony. Before I went, I met a friend in Shaftesbury Square, which is in Belfast City Centre. He knew that I was going to Liverpool and told me that he had a sister who lived there but he'd never met her. "If you see her, will you give her this telephone number and then she can ring me," he said.

I laughed. "Do you know how big Liverpool is?" I replied.

"Please, just take it anyway," he said.

I knew it was a long shot, but I noted his sister's name, wrote down his number on a piece of paper and I put it in my wallet.

I arrived at Liverpool Central Hall for the conference. When it was time, I walked on stage and spoke about my youth, how I ended up in prison, and about the moment I gave my life to Jesus and how God has been working in my life ever since. I was only speaking for about two or three minutes, but unbeknown to me, there was a girl sitting in the audience who was hanging on my every word. As she listened, she wrote a poem about my life.

When the conference was over, the girl came up to me and introduced herself. Then she read out her poem:

> "Today I met a man, who spoke the truth
> Who spoke with the fragmentation of his youth
> Of a land of conflict and judgement misplaced
> Preconceived ideas destroying a race
> But he held high his head and he talked of the day
> That through the confusion, he took life away
> It wasn't a sentimental tale and pity had no place
> It was a humbling story of a God full of grace
> A simple reminder that sin has no size
> Of the quality we share if we look through God's eyes
> We are each of us guilty, but blameless through grace
> Each of us saved through shame and disgrace
> Today I met a man who spoke the truth, but who spoke it out just as it is
> In the knowledge that God's forgiveness is his."

I had never been able to express my story like that. I'd met a girl who understood me.

She went out with me the next day and we sat down at the Mersey. As we looked out, there was a dark cloud over the Mersey, but the sun was breaking through.

"Look, there's the light, the sun is shining," she said.

Then she told me that life hadn't been easy for her either, that she had been adopted and grew up on The Wirral.

She invited me to stay with her for the weekend in Manchester, where she was living at the time. A friend and I travelled to Manchester.

We were approaching a shopping centre and I remembered my promise to my friend back home, so I decided to just go and ask a passer-by.

"Have you heard of this wee girl?" I asked him.

He was very helpful, and even though he didn't know of her, he pointed to a dole office and suggested that I go in and ask there.

I followed his advice and asked one of the assistants. "I hope you don't mind; I'm trying to find this wee girl for a friend of mine. She's his sister and he's never met her."

"We can't give you any information because we're not allowed to do that," the man said.

"I know you're not allowed to give any information out, but if I give you a telephone number, if you do know who this person is, would you tell her to ring that number?" I then relayed the story.

We then continued our journey up to Manchester. Within an hour of arriving at her flat, I had a call; it was the wee girl's mother. She questioned me about her daughter having a brother. I told her that my friend was from Chicago in America, but he had grown up in Northern Ireland. She was understandably upset, so I explained that I wasn't alluding to who the mother or father was. I was simply passing on a message from a friend who said that this girl was his sister.

Two weeks later, the girl came over and my friend met his sister for the first time. From that meeting that I had in Shaftesbury Square, I found out that he had another two brothers, one who lived in Ardoyne, while the other lived in Saintfield, both areas of Belfast. I was able to bring them all together. I believe that it is only God who would do something like that. We serve an incredible God.

Six weeks later, we got married and we settled in Northern Ireland. On January 7, 1997, our daughter was born. The day that she came into the world was probably the happiest day of my life. I think it was the experience of lying in my bed and having my daughter on my chest. I don't think you can describe that feeling.

In the summer, when my daughter was about six months old, my mum died. I had always said to myself that I didn't want my mum to die until my child was born. She had been ill with cancer. I was a Christian at the time and had just got married; everything was going well in my life. My mum was very proud of what I was doing in my life.

Sometime later, we moved to Carrickfergus, a town beside the sea, twelve miles from Belfast, where we lived in a four-bedroom house.

But I began to think that maybe we needed to do something different and have a fresh start. So, I applied for a job in Norwich, in England as a youth pastor. They interviewed me and I got the job. It was the year 2000.

There was a lot of pressure on us at the time. Moving to the east of England and getting settled in brought along its challenges. At least our daughter hadn't started school yet, so it wasn't so unsettling for her.

I was loving my job as a youth pastor and I was doing great work; it was all rosy. I used to go out at 7:30 in the mornings into the city centre. I had a good relationship with all the homeless in the city and often got them breakfast. It was a great way of building bridges and striking up a good rapport with people in the community. I used to go round and see them and let them know that we were there for them.

In the church where I was working, which was the Dereham Road Baptist Church, I used to visit all the neighbours in the area and introduce myself by going round to each door in the community.
That was how I built up relationships with people. For me, it was very successful, but one of the difficulties was that I wasn't used to being with people who drank alcohol and certainly not Christians who drank alcohol.

Sure enough, there were people who were used to having a glass of wine with their meal and there were people who would go out and have a couple of pints of beer at the pub. Previously, I'd had no interest in drink, I'd never really touched drink since my release from prison. Now, don't get me wrong, I didn't go out and get drunk, but I would end up socialising and out of courtesy, I would end up drinking a few pints of beer in an evening. It was all about building up relationships with people and being sociable. However, this was not part of my culture in Northern Ireland. In England, people seemed to drink excessively and then were not in control of their actions. I had a lot of good friendships with all kinds of people from different cultures and backgrounds. I even got to know a magistrate and his partner. I actually ended up doing some work on his house for him.

I used to have a motorcycle to transport me to and from work. One night, I met with two of my friends in a pub, in Norwich. They had bought me a season ticket to watch Norwich play football. On this particular occasion, I drank four pints. I knew what I was doing, but I had gone over the limit. I then drove home, but unfortunately I was hit by an articulated lorry, and I should have died but God had a plan for my life. The police arrived and I was breathalysed. The policeman confirmed that I was over the limit and I was charged with drink driving. Because of the type of person that I was, I felt that I had to resign from my job.

So, I went to the church and I told them everything that had happened.

By this time, I had been working for the church for eighteen months.

To be truthful, they wouldn't have been all that hard on me, but I was harder on myself.

"I don't feel like I have any other option but to resign from my job because I'm working with young people," I said.

"No, we don't want you to resign," one of them replied.

But I couldn't accept that. "No, I have to. At the end of the day, if I'm trying to be a good example to young people, I can't let that happen. So, I'm sorry, but I'm resigning."

I simply couldn't live with myself, never mind anyone else. It really did hurt, but I thought that it was the right thing to do. So, I resigned at the end of 2001 and then I moved back to Manchester with my wife and daughter

Chapter 11
A Downward Spiral

We had decided to move back to Manchester because that was where my wife was from. We bought a four-bedroom house with the sale proceeds of our existing house. It was located just off Moston Lane. It was near to her friends so that at least she would have them close to her. Our relationship though, unfortunately, was beginning to suffer and cracks started to appear in our marriage. I began to think that this was the end of it. It shouldn't have been, but that was the way things were heading.

Nonetheless, the next thing that I needed to do was to get a job to support myself, and my wife and daughter. The first job that I applied for was a door job, working as a doorman in a nightclub.

I went to a club that Bernard Manning owned called The Embassy Club on the Rochdale Road. My friend Jim was from Belfast and that club was his local, he asked me if I would do the door for him. That was my very first job in Manchester. Obviously, I didn't have a door badge that was required at the time.

Nowadays, you have to go on a Door Supervisor Course, which enables you to apply for an SIA Licence, and then you can work legally as a security guard or a door supervisor. But back then, the SIA door badge had not been introduced. You were just certified with a badge from the local council. So, I went to the Manchester City Council to apply for a door badge.

The person in front of me in the queue had been convicted of a driving offence and they turned him down for a door badge. I was beginning to think that I didn't stand a chance with my past conviction, but I was determined to get a job and I realised that I had nothing to lose. So, I went next and was shown into a room where I sat in front of the board. The Chairman looked at me.

"Mr Calderwood, you've been convicted of murder," he said.

"I know," I replied.

He stared at me. "Would you like to explain that to me?"

I thought for a minute and then I spoke. "The only way that I can explain this, is that I lived in Northern Ireland, Belfast. The IRA were killing my people. They were killing British soldiers and police on the streets and they were killing people from my community. All I can say is, that I didn't think that the security forces were doing enough, so I took the law into my own hands and I went out to kill the people who were killing me. That was what my belief was back then. They were murdering us and we were murdering them. They weren't doing enough so that was why there were Loyalist paramilitary organisations. Now, as I stand here today, I truly regret anything that I have been a part of, but that was life in Northern Ireland at the time. I'm living in Manchester now. I've got a wife and a child and I need to look after them. That is the reason that I am applying for a job."

I was sent out of the room as it was obvious that my application needed to be discussed by the board. After some time, I was called back in and they gave me the badge.

As soon as I had a badge, that allowed me to start doing the door. But it was then that my life began to spiral downward.

I had started doing the door for money and this was my very first job in the Rochdale Road. It was something I knew I could do. The hours, of course, were unsociable. I left the house at 4 o'clock in the afternoon and I wouldn't get home until 4 o'clock in the morning. Therefore, I had to sleep all day and my life became this cycle of just bed and work. I was spending more time away from my family and more time away from home. The pressure began to mount because I wasn't able to spend time with my wife and daughter. As a result, I became lost and started drinking and doing drugs.

Working on the door, being a bouncer, is not an easy job. Obviously, you have to look after yourself. It was a downfall for me because I had to protect the door that I was working on at all costs. As with a lot of door work, particularly in nightclubs, there was trouble with gangsters. Consequently, this led to a lot of fighting and arguing, and fighting with other gangs.

At the time, there was a notorious family, called the Noonans. They were one of the big gangster families in Manchester and I became friendly with them.

One of the brothers ran a club called Haçienda which was a well-known nightclub in Manchester. It became famous during the eighties and nineties, and it widened the Manchester house and rave scene. It also had a hand in promoting the music careers of some famous bands and singers, notably, New Order, The Happy Mondays and Oasis. Madonna is also remembered for beginning one of her tours in England by playing in this club. Unfortunately, it also became renowned for increasing the drugs community in Manchester. This was how the Noonan family made their name by starting to work on that door.

The people who I began working with, knew the Noonans. Because of my friendship with one of them, everyone was under the assumption that I was doing the doors in the nightclubs for the Noonans, but I wasn't; I was doing the doors for myself. I was using my contacts with the Noonans, but it was actually me who was running the door.

However, I wasn't going to tell anybody any differently. My thought was that if that's what they wanted to think, then let them think it. If you were associated with the Noonans, then people wouldn't pick a fight with you; they would leave you alone and that suited me.

I had been doing the doors at various different nightclubs and at one particular time, one of the Noonans asked me if I would do a door for him at a nightclub in Stockport. I did the door for six weeks in a row at the weekends. On the seventh week, the Noonan brother said to me, "Alex, I don't want you doing the door for me tonight in Stockport, you're going somewhere else." So, I had the night off that particular club and I ended up working in a different one.

When I do a door, I fulfil my job criteria, which is, if they don't pay on the door, then they're not coming in. Before this happened, there had been a gang coming to the nightclub each week. Cheetham Hill and Moss Side were the two places that these gangs came from. These people would come to the nightclub and say, "Do you know who I am? We don't pay anywhere." But I would say, "If you're coming in, then you're paying. If you're not paying, then you're not coming in."

So, I didn't let them in and they took umbrage at that.

So, I didn't do the door for him that night in Stockport and a gang came to that club and one of the doormen was shot dead, and another one was seriously injured. I don't know if the Noonans knew what was going on, but they knew to get me out of the road.

I think that it was one of those scenarios where a gang had refused to pay and the doormen wouldn't let them in. Those sorts of incidents were happening all the time and were a reflection of life back then.

I believe that God must have had his hand upon my life as I should have been on that door and he made sure that I was out of harm's way.

Although I don't believe that this was God's will for me at the time, but I had wandered away and wasn't listening to God's call on my life. Nevertheless, he still protected me and patiently waited for the day when I would return to him.

Working away from Stockport, led to me getting a job in the heart of Manchester. It was at a nightclub called Lucid which was at the printworks, in the city centre. It happened to be the biggest nightclub in Manchester at the time as it held around 2,500 people. There was a complete diversity of cultures attending this club and everyone wanted to work at it.

I think that I had a wee bit of fortune on my side because the manager of the club was actually from Belfast. "Where are you from big lad?" he said when I went to apply for the job. "I'm from the Shankill," I replied. We got talking and obviously he knew where the Shankill was and he knew a lot of people who I had known. So, I got the job. That was about 2002.

There were a lot of guys working on the doors, but I was the one who ended up taking over that club with the job of head doorman. I worked there for about two and a half years and there were many similar experiences of different gangs trying to get in without paying. As head doorman, I actually had twenty-five doormen working for me. So, it was quite a good job for me and it was a huge responsibility.

I suppose in a sense, everyone thinks that if you're working on the doors then you have to be a hard man; you have to be tough. I think everyone thought that working on the doors meant that you were getting into fights all the time, but that wasn't the case. I found it was always better to articulate your argument rather than fight your argument and my experience working with young people as a youth pastor, helped me. I was good at talking people down and diffusing a situation rather than creating a bigger one.

However, I did begin to wonder how I had got myself into this position; I suppose I've learnt my lesson now. I had to look after myself because, of course, I was in the gangster scene, which often attracts trouble. Maybe, it was God trying to let me know.

During that period of time, I became friendly with another wee lad who'd actually lived in the Unity flats, in the Catholic area in Belfast.

He was called Desmond Priestly or Desi for short. I met up with him, had a good chat and we ended up getting a pub together. It was called The Bricklayers Arms. Desi and I became good friends and the bar we ran was on Moston Lane in Harper-Hay, in the Manchester Rochdale Road area. Just above where Bernard Manning had his club. There was another pub called The Top Derby, and we began running that pub as well.

At the time, you could rent a pub for about £5,000. You also needed somebody who held a licence. We knew a woman who held one, so we paid her to be our licensee.

Eventually, because of my lifestyle of working all night and my drinking, which had become a habit, I was seeing my family less and less, and this led to more difficulties in my marriage. Finally, when we reached the point of no return, me and my wife split up. I offered to give her the house, but she didn't want it. She just took the car and sold it to get herself set up with our daughter.

This happened in 2005, and then in 2006, my father died from ill health. I came back to Belfast for the funeral and then made the decision not to go back to Manchester again. It is possible that my dad may have died from asbestosis, but the hospital didn't want to admit that. He would have caught it when he was working in the shipyard. A lot of men have put forward claims for it since, but my father never received any compensation.

It was a difficult period in my life and because of all this madness that I found myself in, I lost my connection in The Bricklayers Arms and then I lost The Top Derby. It wasn't long before I also lost my house because when I came home, I just didn't go back again. I had no interest in it. But I wasn't worried about that because when I came home, after my father died, I turned to alcohol again for a while because I didn't know where to go. Alcohol became the predominant thing in my life.

I was lost and in a dark place.

I had been living on the Shankill and I got myself a house. For two years or so I was just running about in a daze. It wasn't an easy time.

Because of my drinking and the trauma of losing my family and my businesses, I suffered from heart failure. I was living on Brookmount Street at the time, which was a year after my father passed away. I had been drinking quite heavily. I was in the house one night and I didn't feel right. I wanted to go to the toilet, but I couldn't get out of bed. I managed to get down the stairs and I went to the toilet. I knew that I wasn't going to be able to get back up the stairs again. I phoned an ambulance and put on the hall light. It was one of those narrow streets that I lived on. I opened the front door and as far as I'm aware, when the ambulance came, they found me on the sofa. They took me to the hospital and eventually I recovered. From then on, I have suffered with arrhythmia which is an irregular heartbeat. I live with this now and am aware that this is a result of the drinking problem that I had.

When I eventually got back on my feet, I met an old friend in Belfast called Billy. He asked me how I was and I told him how I had got into drinking.

"Why don't you come and stay with me and have a holiday?" he said. My friend owned a pub in Bournemouth. I really needed a break so I took him up on his invitation.

When he got back, he sent me some money in the post to pay for my travel. I arranged to stay with Billy for two weeks. The pub was called Deacons in Bournemouth on the Christchurch Road.

There were two other men staying in the pub with Billy, both were called Martin. One of the guys was Irish and an ex-soldier. The other guy was English and worked for Billy in the pub.

Unbeknown to me, the two Martins went out and committed the robbery of a snooker hall in the local area. After the robbery, Billy and I were charged with conspiracy. Obviously, I knew Billy. He was my friend from Belfast who had invited me over, but I had never met the two Martins before.

The two Martins were both caught, and they pleaded guilty. The strange thing is, that it meant that they were not allowed to be at my trial or Billy's. But they both made it very clear in their statements that they had done the robbery and that me and Billy had nothing to do with it.

They said that I had left the door open for them to rob the place, but that is simply not true because I didn't even want to go to the snooker hall. And that was made very clear at the trial.

When I was arrested at the pub, the policeman found money in my bedroom. "I believe this is your cut from the robbery," the policeman said. "Well, I can assure you that money is nothing to do with the robbery," I replied. I told them exactly where I had got the money. I had placed £10 as a bet on Steven Gerrard. My bet was that Steven Gerrard would score the first goal in the England match, and they won 3–1. I won the bet and also £510. I told the policeman about the bet.

"I can check that out you know," he replied. "Believe me, I want you to check it out and then you'll know that I'm not telling you lies."

While I was awaiting my trial, I went to the manager of William Hill, the bookmakers. He gave me a copy of my bookie docket to prove where my money came from. They didn't check it out and then they said in court that it was the money from the robbery. I produced the ticket. "Well, that's not an issue anymore," they said.

"Mr Calderwood, we had a look at your Ericsson phone, but we couldn't download any messages from it," the prosecutor said.

"That's because you don't get the messages from an individual mobile phone, you get the messages from the network," I replied in disbelief.

I had nothing to hide, so I had given them my phone. I could have got rid of it, but I didn't and I told them what content my messages contained. I knew that there wasn't anything on my phone that connected me to anything.

There were so many inconsistences that happened during the trial surrounding the evidence. After the trial, I rang the phone network and I asked them if they gave a copy of my messages to the police. I was informed that my question couldn't be answered and that I would have to talk to my solicitor. I told them that I was a customer and that I was simply asking a question. Unfortunately, they wouldn't give me an answer.

When they found me guilty of the robbery, they gave me my £510 back again — the money that they had originally claimed was a cut from the robbery. I couldn't make any sense out of it all. When the trial ended, the Jjudge ordered the immediate destruction of all the evidence. I've never known that to happen before and now I am determined to fight to clear my name.

I spoke to one of the Martins because I'm still trying to get my case back to court. I have always denied that I was involved in a conspiracy.

Martin and I will make a statement to a solicitor to say that I did not have any involvement with the robbery. Our argument is that Martin should have been brought into court to testify my innocence at the time.

Once this is done, my intention will be to take it to the police and complain about my wrongful conviction. I am determined to pursue it and I won't let it go until the day I die.

Chapter 12

Seeds of Hope

As the hammer went down in court, I could not believe that here I was again. I was facing a sentence of seven years. Only this time, it was different; I knew that I was innocent. The odds had been stacked against me. They had looked at my past conviction and jumped to conclusions. I felt that I had been incriminated with manufactured evidence — my associations with who I was staying with, my winnings, alleged messages on my phone and my past.

Just when I didn't think things could get any worse, more difficulties were thrown my way. False accusations and family tragedy were among the bitter pills I had to swallow.

I began my sentence in 2008, at HMP Dorchester in Dorset. I was only there for five months and was about to experience more disruption when I spent another five months at each of three different prisons. From Dorchester, I was sent to HMP Wymott, near Leyland in Lancashire, and then I was moved to HMP Garth, which is also in Lancashire.

HMP Garth was a difficult time because there was an outstanding charge that I'd had from about three and a half years previously. I had been arrested for an assault on a policeman. But the policeman was the one that had actually hit me. Apparently, he thought that I was going to hit him, so he hit me. Although, I didn't hit anybody. But they didn't do anything about it at that time. Then out of the blue, they suddenly decided to charge me with assault on a police officer. And that's when they transferred me back to HMP Maghaberry, in Northern Ireland.

When I went to court for the alleged assault on a policeman, the judge said, that it was an abusive process. "Why have you waited so long to charge this man?" he asked. He threw the case out of court, so to speak, and gave me a complete discharge.

Somehow, this turned out to be a blessing in disguise, and proved that God still had his hand on my life.

What I didn't know at the time, was that my sister Elizabeth, the second eldest in our family, had cancer and was in hospital. So, as I had been transferred back to Maghaberry Prison where I was able to apply for compassionate leave.

Two prison officers brought me out so that I could visit her in the hospital. It wasn't long after that when she passed away. I realised that it was a Godsend that I was back in Northern Ireland and at least I could go and see her before she died. It was a great blessing because I would have hated not to have seen her before she died. I am very comfortable with the fact that she was a Christian and so I believe that she is in a better place. Elizabeth passed into glory in 2010.

At the end of the day, I was happy. I was happy and sad at the same time I suppose. I was happy that I'd been able to see my sister, but I was sad that she had died.

Sometime later, while I was still at Maghaberry, I received a letter from an old friend; Anne Gallagher. I hear you say, Who is Anne Gallagher? Well, her brothers were more well-known in the Troubles than Anne, in fact, one would find it difficult to believe they came from the same family.

Anne's family was from Bellaghy, county Londonderry, where the IRA was always strong. Her brothers were part of the IRA. Her brother Dominic, *Mad Dog* McGlinchey, who claimed to have killed thirty-one people including a child, was an IRA combatant who fought alongside Francis Hughes,[19] later Mad Dog would swap and lead the INLA[20] and in 1994, he was shot dead by his ex-associates.

Anne's other brother, Sean McGlinchey, served eighteen years in prison for his part in the bombing of Coleraine town when six people were murdered. Only in Northern Ireland could terrorists be elected for government. Imagine USA citizens electing or having to elect al-Qaeda terrorists who orchestrated 9–11. Somehow here on the island of Ireland, the Republican side still glorifies terrorism. Even as I write this, social media is showing young adult Catholics singing RA[21] songs at a festival to celebrate Irish culture. These are people who were born after the Troubles, but are still being fed political propaganda without realising that the very people they are singing about, were the very people who killed the most Catholics — yes, they executed their own.

I first met Anne in 1996, when I was working on the Shankill, doing cross-community work with people from the Shankill and the Falls (included Ardoyne and Newtownabbey.) One day, I was on the Shankill and this girl walked towards me. I spoke to her and she shared her vision of bringing the Loyalists and the Republican prisoners together. It was an initiative that she called Seeds of Hope. She knew lots of ex-Loyalist prisoners. I was working for the Probation Board at the time and I ran the Shankill Road Youth Club for the Belfast Education and Library Board. It was around that time that I struck up a friendship with her. Anne was a nurse in the Royal Victoria Hospital.

Because of the hard reality of what her brothers had been involved in, Anne had a vision. She could not see any sense in all the killing and

---

19 Described by RUC Chief Constable Kenneth Newman as *The most wanted man in the North*. Dominic was the second hunger striker to die in the H-Block hunger strike.
20 Formed in 1974, after parting ways from the IRA.
21 IRA songs.

she was inspired to search for answers. She wanted to try and help people, by deterring them from killing others. She believed that if she could eradicate the line between the division, then this would be a step forward towards peace. Her vision was not to necessarily unite the two sides, but to develop relationships between the opposed, to understand each other and begin to build bridges.

One way of doing this, she believed, was to bring ex-prisoners together, (the UDA, UVF and IRA, INLA, etc) to communicate and have meetings with each other and to work out the best way to move forward together. This is what the organisation of Seeds of Hope was all about.

Anne told me that she wanted me to take her to meet with those across the fence. I took her to speak with the leader of the UVF. I introduced her to him and she revealed her vision. Anne has since been responsible for bringing a lot of people together.

Through my friendship with Anne, I met Patrick Magee. Patrick had been involved in the Brighton Grand Hotel bombing of 1984. The bombing killed five people, including Conservative MP, Sir Anthony Berry. Anne got Patrick and Sir Anthony's daughter, Joanne Berry, together. They formed a friendship and then travelled around and gave speeches and presentations about their friendship.

Anne asked me to take part in some of those events. I became involved and worked on the vision with her. At one time, she asked me to come down to one of the meetings in Dublin where Patrick and Joanne would be speaking. I went, met them both and helped out at the event.

As a result of these meetings, Anne's vision for Seeds of Hope grew.

She went on to do a lot of work with ex-prisoners and became very good at getting them together. Years later, when I was in Maghaberry Prison, in 2010, I was still in contact with Anne. She wrote to me while I was in prison to try and get me to come and work with her again as soon as I got out …

"Dear Oso,

I seem to start my letters to you with sorry, and I know how much it means to prisoners to receive a letter. I'm sure Ronnie has told you I had a car accident which was a blessing in disguise to doing Seeds of Hope. If you can organise a visit before the end of August, I will let you know all the good things that have been happening and one is the Clock Project. I know you will be getting out soon and you need a job. I am putting an application together for the Department of Foreign Affairs and I want to apply for core funding for project workers. I want you and Ronnie to be project coordinators for Seeds of Hope. You are the right person for that and I believe your heart wants to make a difference and so does Ronnie. I know you will be getting out soon. My brother Sean was made Mayor in Limavady which is in the area of Coleraine where he got 19 years for the Coleraine Bomb. Two of the people who came out to support him, one of them lost her mother, she was only 30 years old and the other lady's aunt was Mayor of Coleraine at the time and was killed. Jean Jefferson was her name and wants to be involved in Seeds of Hope. I have organised a Seeds of Hope conference next weekend in Donegal, and Jean is coming to give a talk on the importance of moving on. This lady called Mary Noble contacted me from America, she wanted to come and interview me about Seeds of Hope. I was not interested in that, but when I Googled her, I was really interested in what she did internationally so I decided to organise a group of people around what she did. I am having the week away in a beautiful heritage centre in Donegal where 17 years ago was the first weekend of Seeds of Hope. I have been offered one acre of land there to develop the Seeds of Hope, yellow & red. Rose and Jeff Barr from the Koran Centre in Strabane have given one acre of land, also to develop the Seeds of Hope Rose. You probably are reading this and thinking I have heard all this before. Yes, you have, but this time it is 17 years on and so many ironic points have been gained. I am doing the white caller boxing tournament in October. Battle of the Mayors. Between Sean and the Mayor of Letterkenny. Both shared a cell in Long Kesh years ago. I hope you realise at this point I am not going to give up on you and the concept of Seeds of Hope.
Lots of love Anne."

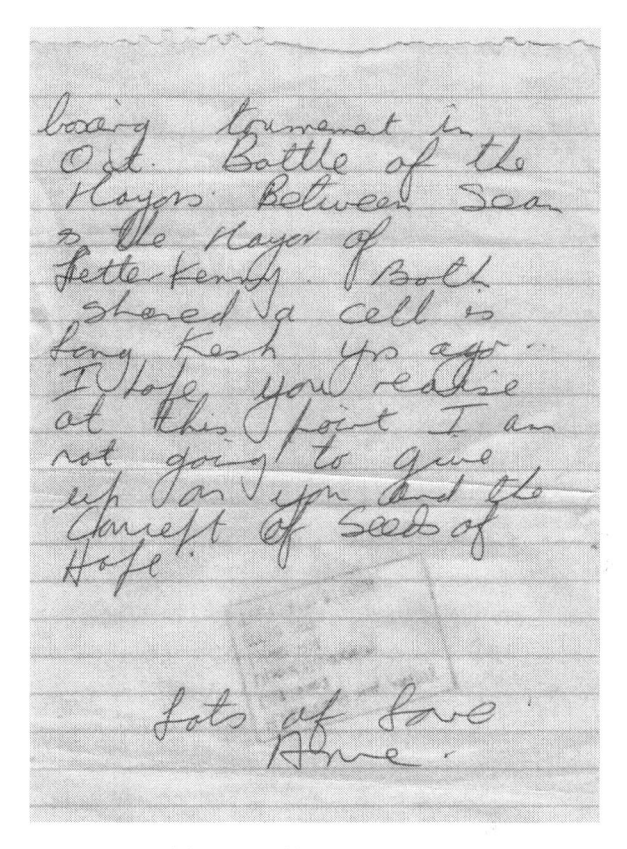

The last page of the original letter. Note: Prison stamp on it.

Anne was basically saying that she hadn't forgotten about me and she knew what it was that I wanted to do. Anne inspired me to hang on in there until I eventually came out.

Maghaberry Prison was where I finished off my sentence. I had completed four and a half years of my sentence and I came out in 2012.

I stayed on probation for a very long time. I hadn't even been given a probation order; I was just given a seven-year sentence.

The probation ran a prison work-out scheme and it was to help you to integrate into the community again. The work-out scheme was called

Extern. In the scheme, prisoners are allowed to come out of prison to work for the day. We were driven out in a minibus and got involved in different activities. There was an opportunity to do a lot of sewing, by making blankets and so on. I got involved in upholstery. Every day I worked until about 3 p.m. and then we had to drive back to the prison.

So, that would be my activity in the daytime from Monday to Friday.

On the Friday at 1 p.m., instead of going back to the prison on the bus, we were dropped off in the city centre and allowed to go home for the weekend. So, that was what the scheme entailed; it equipped you with useful skills so that you would be able to get a job more easily and be less likely to re-offend. This lasted for about a year in 2011, and it was also when I started coming back into the church and the café.

Let me finish this chapter with a thought from Anne …

"We encourage people not to judge others. We listen to people's stories, but we don't judge them. There's healing in that. The idea is that when you hear my story and I hear your story, it becomes our story, and seeds of hope are sown."

Chapter 13
The Prodigal Returns

It was 2017. I had been out of prison for five years on probation, but I still felt like a lost soul. I had fallen away from the Lord and was still drinking, doing drugs and gambling. Nothing made any sense anymore and I was very unhappy.

I didn't believe it was right that I was on probation for so long. The probation officers said that it was part of my life sentence because I hadn't served it previously. That was why they tried to monitor me and tried to criminalise me. "You can't criminalise me when I've already served my sentence. Why have I been on probation for so long? If you don't sort this out then I'm going to kill myself. I'm coming down to tell you that I'm going to kill myself and I'll hold you responsible,' I said to them at the time.

When I told them that, they had me released within two weeks.

My routine was to go down to the New Life City Church, to the café, which was called, The Olive Branch. This was used as a drop-in centre, for people aged from eighteen to seventy to call in for a cup of tea or coffee and to have a chat. This could be for social purposes or to discuss day-to-day problems. The church ran many programmes in the building, which was a very effective outreach as many were delivered on a cross-community basis.

One morning, when I was walking down Northumberland Street,

which leads to the café, I started thinking about my whole life: about my childhood, my teenage years, prison, release, marriage, having a baby, going to England as a youth pastor, Manchester, the gangs and gangsters, and back to prison again. I was tired of everything that the world had to offer. I was tired of doing drink and drugs, and partying.

If I am truthful, it created a way of living that involved depression, loneliness, low self-esteem and suicidal thoughts. The ultimate question that I was left with was, what is life all about?

The one thing that I hadn't realised when I was a Christian was that I was happy. I had a family, I had plenty of fellowship and there was joy and there was peace. Believe me, these are not merely words; it was the reality of my life at that particular time. I was surrounded by many genuine friends.

As I continued to walk towards the café, I began to cry. I thought, *Oso, you've been here before; you don't know where your life is*. I felt utterly confused as if I had reached a dead end. I cried out to the Lord and asked him to help me. In a moment, a verse from the Bible came to my mind, it was 1 John, 1:9, *If we confess our sins, he is faithful and just to forgive us our sins and cleanse us from all unrighteousness.* (NKJV) Then another verse came to me: *Trust in the Lord with all your heart and lean not on your own understanding. In all your ways acknowledge him and he will direct your paths.* Proverbs 3: 5–6, NKJV.

As I pondered those verses, I continued to cry, but I finally walked into the church, sat down and had a cup of coffee. I thought to myself, *the Christian life is not an easy life*. I was obviously going through ups and my downs like everyone else. I knew that following Jesus was the right path to choose and I hoped that from now on, I would always put God first in my life. I decided to seek to obey him and I really didn't want to upset anyone with my demeanour or my actions.

I spoke to a couple of men at the church who were both Christians and they gave me support and prayed with me.

I thought about St Paul who said in the Bible, *I do not understand what I do. For what I want to do I do not do, but what I hate I do. And if I do what I do not want to do, I agree that the law is good.* Romans 7:15–20, NIV. I felt that I could really identify with that verse. I believe that for many years, my life was caught up in that trap. I wanted to do what was right, but I kept doing things that were wrong. I couldn't understand what was going on. I was really depressed during those years. It was more of an existence rather than living a life. Obviously, I have a lot of regrets because when I got out of prison in 1993, I had everything going for me. I had a wife, I had a child, I had my own house and I had a good job. I had been given everything that the world had to offer me, but when I look back on it, the reality was that I didn't accept my blessings. When I began drinking again, even though it was on a social basis, my body couldn't cope with it.

I've learnt that it's a good place to just start from where you are. I still have the urge to occasionally go and have a drink. I happen to live near a pub, so I'll call in sometimes just to say hello to friends and they ask me if I'm going to have a drink, but I have to be strong and say no. It is a constant battle that I have every day. Sometimes you can be sitting on your own and it's hard, but I need to be strong and trust in God.

The key factor in all this is that my aim is to be a good example to other people. So, I know that I can't be a good witness to people if I'm seen in a pub or if I'm seen in a bookies or if I'm seen doing anything that can take me off the track of leading a good life. I really want to be what God wants me to be; that's what I'm striving for and that's what I'm praying about.

There are times when I am attacked with feelings of guilt. One guy once said to me, "I thought you were a Christian." "I am a Christian," I replied "Well, what are you doing drinking then?" he added.

Now, there's no way that I'm going to justify having an alcoholic drink.

I have friends who are alcoholics so there's no way that I'm going to proclaim that it's alright to have a pint because I know that an alcoholic won't stop there. It is a difficult one. I think that the company you keep will dictate the kind of person that you are. It's important to me because I want to be honest with all the people from the Shankill who will read this book. I would like to say to anyone I know, that if I have offended you by going out and having a drink, then I apologise.

I understand that I have led a terrible life, a really bad life.

When I look at the news and see devastation, war, and people getting killed, it is really upsetting. On the other hand, I can sit in the house on a Saturday night and watch The X-Factor and start crying when somebody's singing.

All I can do now is ask God to help me and pray that He will guide and direct me into living my life in the right way. I still feel guilty because I've wasted of a lot of years. Although, I'm not worried about myself, I feel as if I've wasted these years for God and I'd like to make amends for that now by doing good.

I have said it before and I say it again, everyone is human and we all make mistakes, including you. The sadness is that as human beings we measure mistakes … that person's mistake is worse than mine, and so forth. Yet the Bible says, *For ALL have sinned, and come short of the glory of God.* Romans 3:23, KJV.

Oso carrying the cross through loyalist and republican areas of Belfast

There was a lot of hurt, a lot of pain, and a lot of frustration throughout my past. Sometimes, you say the wrong thing, but you go away and you think about it and you rectify yourself. The Christian life is not a set of dos and don'ts. I don't think that people always realise what you've been through and sometimes you make mistakes. I want people to realise that they're not alone. I know that Christ is the answer to all my problems and sometimes I go the wrong way, so I get on my knees and talk to God because he's my Heavenly Father and he listens to what I have to say.

In the meantime, I'm still involved with the church, I'm still leading sessions with sectarianism, racism and similar topics, so I'm still very much involved. Occasionally, I'm asked to run sessions and I'll tell a story. So, even if it's my life's testimony, then I'll tell people that. I think it's still important to let people know about the mistakes that you've made because a lot of people like me will say, God will never forgive me for this or God will never forgive me for that, and I say, 'Yes God will forgive you, no matter how many times you did wrong.'

If you believe in God, then you'll want for nothing. As it says in the book of Philippians 4:19, *And my God shall supply all your needs according to His riches in glory by Christ Jesus.* (NKJV.)

I think it's important because a lot of people out there know that I've made mistakes, but it's important to be honest.

I am glad that there is a God and that he intervened in my life. What I would like to say to the people of my community, is that I know that I've not been a great example of what a Christian is supposed to be, and I need to be truthful about that, but I just thank God that I'm not the person that I was.

When I sit on my own, I think about my friends and those with paramilitary backgrounds and they've all come to faith. But the Christian life is not easy because there are so many temptations out there and … *the devil walks about like a roaring lion, seeking whom he may devour.* 1 Peter 5:8, NKJV.

I feel sad in a sense because when I came out of prison in 1993, there seemed to be more Christians around who I could have fellowship with.

In my first flat when I got out, I used to have about fifteen people come round for the weekend. People gave their testimonies; someone gave a reading from scripture. I don't know whether it's because of Covid, but this sort of thing doesn't happen anymore. And I think that is what we need to get back to.

My friend Thomas and I, opened up in church during the Covid pandemic to allow people to come and get a warm drink in a friendly place and have a good chat. It's a wide-open space so that we can all spread out and it was open during most of the Covid season. A lot of people lived on their own and felt isolated. So, this has been a way of getting people together. It's given people a point of contact.

All I want to do is be a good example for the Lord Jesus Christ and that's all I really want for my life. I'm asking people from my community, when you're looking for God or Christianity, don't look to me, look to Christ as he is, *the author and finisher of our faith.* Hebrews 12:2, NKJV.

Christ won't let you down but people will. Keep your eyes on him.

I like this quote from the book of Romans in the Bible, 10:13, ... *For whosoever shall call upon the name of the Lord will be saved.* (KJV). I like it that my name can be found in wh<u>oso</u>ever.

Sadly, there are a few people in this area who have taken their own lives recently, including a couple of my personal friends, and I wonder why they didn't choose to speak to someone to see if they could get help. There is one person who sat in our church for about five weeks and then the next thing I heard was that he had committed suicide.

 I want to be available to help people even if they just need a chat to talk about their problems. If I can explain how God is willing to help and protect people in all situations, then that is a bonus and indeed every Christian's calling.

I do believe that God was protecting me, even before I gave my life to Christ, in many different ways. I could share many stories where God has looked after me. I would like to share the following stories — I was sitting in my house one day, worrying that I didn't have any money to pay my gas bill, when a friend sent me a message on social media. It was someone I knew from Scotland. He said to me, "Oso, I've put a wee gift in the bank for you. Get yourself a Chinese." He did the same thing again the very next day. I went to the bank to check and there was £50. So, I decided to get myself some breakfast from the local café when two men walked in. One of them, who I knew from the past, said, "Oso, give me your bank details." I did and he transferred £100 to my account. So, I bought breakfast for him and his son.

I walked down to the church and another man messaged me to say, "Do me a favour, send me your bank details." "What for?" I replied. And he said, "Send me your bank details, I haven't seen you for a while."

Then he messaged to say that he'd sent me a gift of £200.

As I sat in church, reflecting on God's goodness, I saw a girl who was a frequent visitor. She thought she was suffering from a satanic attack.

I asked another church member to come and I said, "We'll pray with you." I asked her if she was hungry to which she nodded. So, I said, "Come on, I'll get you some dinner." God allows you to do that. I haven't worked in eight years, but I don't need the work as the time isn't right yet. God will let me know when that time comes.

Oso helping to complete forms

The following week, the same thing happened again. A friend said, "Give me your bank details." "What for?" I said. "Because my boyfriend says that he wants to give you a wee gift. So, give me your bank details," she replied. This was in July of last year, 20z21. Ever since I came out of prison, God has continued to look out for me, even when I have fallen away from Him.

Recently, I met a man who was a minister in Manchester, when I was there. He's back home again, but he's lost his leg and the toes on his other foot. He's had cancer and a stroke and as a result, also lost half of his jaw. When I found out that he was home, I phoned him and met up with him for coffee in the city centre. "What is it that you want to do?" I asked him. He said that he'd love to work with ex-prisoners which was really encouraging and he was needed in our community.

But the day after I met him he was back in hospital again. "Oso, the doctor thinks that I've got an infection in my bones so, I'm going to be in here for nine months," he said. "No, you're not going to be here for nine months. What you need to do is pray and I'll pray too," I replied. It turned out that he was in hospital for only three weeks. It's things like that, that tell me God had a hand in this life.

After all that has happened in my life, I am open to God's calling and wherever He calls me, I am willing to go.

The Cross Walk

As I walk along the Shankill
And I walk along the Falls
And I think of the old times
Where we all had our fun

Well, we all played together
There were very simple games
Kick the Tin, or Arallyo
We all played these games

Then in 1969, when everything changed
It was then came divisions
And our friendship, was never the same

Then for thirty years of conflict
There was pain, tears and death
What were our reasons
What was all this fighting for

Now there's one more thing to say now
After all these troubled years
Let's not forget the victims
As all the pain is the same

As I walk along the Shankill
And I walk along the Falls
Well, it's just like the old times
Where we can play our games again.

(Written outside prison)

CONTACT THE AUTHOR

To invite Oso to share his story please contact the publisher.

INSPIRED TO WRITE A BOOK?

Contact
Maurice Wylie Media
Inspirational & Christian Book Publisher

Based in Northern Ireland and distributing around the world.
www.MauriceWylieMedia.com

Printed in Great Britain
by Amazon